Adolf
Hitler's
Ghost

Adolf Hitler's Ghost

Elizabeth Maria Schmid, M.D.

ARPress
ILLUMINATING IDEAS.
EMPOWERING VOICES.

ARPress
45 Dan Road Suite 5
Canton, MA 02021

Hotline: 1(888) 821-0229
Fax: 1(508) 545-7580

Ordering Information:
Quantity sales. Special discounts are available on quantity purchases by corporations,associations, and others. For details, contact the publisher at the address above.

Printed in the United States of America.

ISBN-13:   Softcover   979-8-89389-382-3
               eBook   979-8-89389-381-6

Library of Congress Control Number: 2024916564

Contents

Foreword

This is my autobiography in which I am trying to show how the experiences of World War II and the postwar period with the remaining Nazi and upcoming Neo-Nazi movement influenced my life, even though I was then only a young child. My family is not Jewish, but we were still profoundly touched by Adolf Hitler's dictatorship with my father having to spend several years at the Russian Front, fighting for the German Army, and then paying the price for the war crimes which others had committed, in Sowjet prison camps for five years. In the meantime, I grew up thinking that my father was dead. My family has been Austrian for many centuries, but we were forced to become "Germans" by Hitler. The Neo-Nazi movement, which, unfortunately, is becoming more powerful not only in Germany and Austria, seems to be threatening the entire world today in the form of dictatorships. Only the names of the regimes have changed, but otherwise they are as evil as Adolf Hitler's dictatorship was. Let my writing be a warning to every human being!

This book is dedicated to all people living in dictatorships, in wars, or in fear of having to live in a dictatorship in the near future.

When Adolf Hitler invaded and occupied Austria in spring 1938 (I was 18 months old), every Austrian citizen had to produce a proof of their "Aryan" ancestry. So, my Mutti (Mom) began collecting family histories and searched old parish records from the villages, where our ancestors had come from. In the past, the most reliable records were made and kept by the local parish priests in their parishes. On my father's side she found data going back to 1762, when my father's great-great-grandfather was born in the village of Mariahilf near the capital of Moravia, Znaim, in the Austro-Hungarian Monarchy. His last name was Welzel. He was a farmer who rented a portion of a large farm from his local landlord. In those days, most farmers rented their land for which they had to pay rent and deliver a portion of their harvest. They all spoke German, not a Slavic language, and supposedly were proud of being of Germanic stock. After the "Seven Years' War" between the Austrian Empress Maria Theresia and the Prussian King Friedrich II in the mid-18th century, there had been a massive migration of the people of Eastern Europe according to the principle "Cuius Regio-eius religio" (who owns the land—determines the religion). Most Catholics went into the southern parts of Bohemia, Moravia, Poland, owned by the Habsburg Monarchy, whereas most Protestants had to go north into the lands held by the Prussian King. We assume that our ancestors too had been among those who had migrated into the Catholic Monarchy. The names of the girls' families, whom the Welzel men married, were such as Bachhaimer, Hartl, Flassak, Pfaffstetter, Suchheimer.

All these families used to have many children, because of the high child mortality. One of his sons was Andreas Welzel who, by then, owned his own farm. One of his sons was Karl Wetzel, who had 13 children with his wife, eight of whom survived. Of these surviving children, another Karl Welzel became the chauffeur (horse and carriage) of the well-known Count Schoenborn near Vienna. Later he bought a restaurant from the count of Vienna. The family myth reports very friendly relations with the Schoenborn family, who possibly launched them into the restaurant business in Vienna, and one of them supposedly owned the famous coffeehouse "Fenstergucker" in Vienna. This coffeehouse used to be frequented by many intellectuals and artists and is even mentioned in some novels written by Viennese authors. One of his daughters married a cellist with the Vienna Philharmonics, which was and is a highly regarded position in Vienna. As a Philharmonic he had a good salary, but, unfortunately, he put all his money into a Swiss Bank account. When he died in 1974, he was my father's uncle, nobody could find the account number of his bank, which means that several millions of Austrian money remains on an unknown Swiss Bank account. Another daughter of Karl Welzel married Anton Koller, a violinmaker, who took care of the violins of the Vienna Philharmonics and travelled with them, wherever they had to go to perform. My own father was initially supposed to learn the trade of violinmaking from his Uncle Koller, but he turned out differently. One son of Andreas Koller, born in 1880, became the family "outlaw" by becoming a seaman and working on merchant boats between America and northern Germany. Supposedly, he also lived in America for a while. I remember that I met him once as a little girl, after he had settled down in Bremerhaven. Another son was Johann Welzel, my father's father, born in 1876 near Vienna. He was supposed to become a Catholic priest, but instead attended a teacher's training college in Vienna. I remember him telling us how hungry he had been most of that time. He started with a mini salary as an assistant teacher in a two-class elementary school in a small village near Vienna. He married Katharina Goldschmied, my grandmother, also a schoolteacher. It seems that her name is Jewish, very little is written about her ancestry in our official Ancestry Table. She came probably from a Jewish family who had centuries ago converted to the Catholic faith—they did not have any other chances, if they wanted to stay alive. It may be her genetic contribution to increase the family IQ by many points, because both her sons became academics, my Uncle Robert a medical doctor, and my father Hans a pharmacist.

The Welzel Family

I remember both my paternal grandparents very well. They lived in a small town, Korneuburg at the Danube. It was not easy to visit them by public transportation after the war, and also they lived in the Russian occupation zone after the war and we had to carry identification cards which were strictly controlled by the Russians. This was in the late 40s and early 1950s. Oma and Opa (the German words for granddaddy and grandmom) were classical examples of the class of the petit bourgeois (lower-middle class) and were proud of it. After all, they had been socially upward from their backgrounds as farmers. They lived very frugally, lived in little towns in little houses with little gardens. During the war they raised rabbits and would slaughter one each time when we visited. Since meat was hardly available at that time, it was a feast, a well-prepared rabbit. They also grew grapes in their garden from which they made wine. My Mutti used to say that it was probably the worst wine ever made in the history of winemaking. I have good memories of these visits; my sister Elfi and I would walk down to the Danube and play in the water and sand there or we would sit in a corner of their garden with coffee (not real coffee, which was not available at that time) on warm summer afternoons with mosquitos humming, and listening to the wonderful, melancholy songs from their homeland sung by the Russian soldiers who were quartered in a nearby garrison. "How beautifully the Russians are singing!"—they too, like the German prisoners of war in Russia, must have felt very lonesome and longing for their homelands.

My mother's side of the family goes all the way back into the late 1600s. They all lived in Moravia, like my father's ancestors. This was Habsburg land, strictly Catholic. Most of them had been farmers, some of them had additional skills like beekeeping or weaving or managing an inn. The Tauchmann branch of my mother's family moved from Moravia to the southeast of the land of Steiermark (Styria), near the Hungarian border. This is within the German-speaking portion of the Monarchy, today's Austria. The time was under Emperor Joseph II, the son of the Empress Maria Theresia in the late 1700s. There is a story about a "one-woman pioneer." She was married to a farmer in Moravia and for some unknown reason she left him with their two children to join her relatives in that part of Steiermark where the Tauchmann family lived. The problem was that she was so poor that

5

she had to make her journey by sitting in front of churches and beg for money. My grandmother sometimes pointed out a church in her neighborhood, a beautiful Neo Gothic church, "Votivkirche," where she supposedly had to beg. One reason why the Tauchmann family settled in that part of eastern Austria might have been the fact that land was cheap there and very fertile and the climate almost perfect. Up until 1682, the population in that part of Austria had frequently been killed and their lands destroyed by marauding Turks who used to come up from Hungary, until they were finally defeated by the Empress's general, Prince Eugen of Savoy, who pushed the Turks out of Hungary and even out of Belgrade in Serbia. So this land needed to be repopulated by German farmers and was probably affordable. All these people became wealthy farmers and owned their own lands in a village named "Tautendorf."

One Johann Tauchmann married a Josephine Schnepf, the neighbor's daughter, and they had twelve children. I was told that in those days, sometimes women gave birth directly in the fields where they worked, and resumed work soon thereafter. Josephine Tauchmann is my great-grandmother. I have a photo of her and my grandmother, and my mother holding me as a one- or two-year-old child. This photo must have been taken in 1938. My great-grandmother must have been well over eighty years at that time. She was a stout woman, dressed like a farmer, but with an intelligent face, a fine nose, regular features, still a good-looking woman. It is said that my great-grandfather was quite autocratic, very smart, the mayor of his village, but a real tyrant with his family.

From glimpses of conversation overheard between my grandmother and my mother, I learned some of the family lore.

For instance, my grandmother was a very good student in grade school and her teachers implored her father to let her go to a teachers' training college nearby. But her father would not allow it; it was a luxury for a girl to be educated since she was going to marry a farmer and only needed to know about farming and the upkeep of a house which in those days was not at all an easy job. There was no water inside the houses, water had to be carried in a pail from an outdoor well. There was, of course, no central heating, but one woodstove in the kitchen on which everything was cooked and at the same time it heated the entire house sufficiently. The bedrooms, however, were so cold and unheated that perishable food was stored in the bedrooms. The first thing a farmer's wife had to do in the mornings was to go outside to collect kindling for the stove in order to prepare breakfast. My grandmother had many siblings, of whom six survived and whom I knew. My grandmother, Josephine, escaped the drudgery of farming and married a Johann Posch from a nearby village who was a trained shoemaker. I heard a rumor that my grandfather was not her great love. He had been a village boy who was killed while poaching—apparently he had no license to hunt which was reserved for rich businessmen or the aristocracy. Johann Posch, however, was quite adventurous. He moved to Vienna and with my grandmother's dowry he rented a shoe store and an apartment right above the store in an elegant district of Vienna—at that time that was more adventurous than emigrating to America today. Eventually, they both did very well in Vienna, he repairs shoes and she takes care of the store and they were able to send both of their children, my mother and her brother to private, Catholic schools. And my uncle to the University to study Medicine.

Posch Family, 1924

My Oma (grandmother) moved to Vienna after the wedding, and I know she hated Vienna wholeheartedly. Here was this country girl who had lived mostly outdoors, had been famous for climbing trees better than most of the boys, of riding horses without a saddle like an American Indian, suddenly being confined to a small apartment in Vienna, which was dark because all the windows in the living area went out into a small courtyard. Sometimes travelling organ players would come and play in these courtyards and people would throw some pennies to the little monkey sitting on the organ. The windows of Opas (grandfather's) well-lighted work area went out into Liechtensteinstrasse, a fine street in the 9th district. But this is where Opa and his assistants worked, literally day and night. My Oma had to run down the stairs, each time the bell rang announcing the arrival of a customer in addition to doing all the paperwork, selling shoes, and doing her household duties. She was, by the way, an excellent cook, and I remember watching her making thin noodles from scratch and the famous Vienna apple strudel, which demanded the dough to be stretched paper-thin. It seems that she was well liked by her customers, many of whom were Jewish. My mother was born in 1912, before the First World War. My grandfather was drafted and was one of the soldiers at the infamous Insonzobattles in northern Italy. During and after that war, the civilian population had to suffer more of food shortage than during the Second World War. And then there was the Influenza Epidemic at the end of the war. My grandmother sent my mother and her little brother to her village in East Styria so that they could live with their grandmother in Tautendorf. My mother spoke of these years in the country as "the golden years of her life." She was her grandmother's favorite grandchild and also happened to be very pretty, judging from old photographs, blonde hair, blue eyes and a beautiful face which she retained for the rest of her life.

When she had to return to Vienna, soon after the war, she had to start elementary school. She too hated every moment in that dark apartment, and it seems that both she and her mother suffered of depressions. Maybe some genetic factors, an unhappy marriage, poor nutrition, lack of freedom. They did not know that Dr. Sigmund Freud lived just around the corner, but they would not have gone to see a psychiatrist anyway.

My mother told me that her mother could not get out of bed for about one year due to severe depression. How the family managed is still a puzzle to me. My mother was perhaps eleven or twelve years old. The only thing they could do was pray as devout Catholics. My mother also had to take care of shopping and cooking and cleaning—in her Catholic desperation she even wrote a letter to then famous saint, Therese von Connersreuth, who, supposedly, healed illnesses. It worked! Soon after that my Oma recovered and from then on managed her life competently.

FRANZ THURMAN

11

Maria Posch - Dr. Hans

My Earliest Memories

I was born one year after my parents got married, on August 31, 1936. At that time, we lived in a small apartment in Steingasse, in the 3rd district. Even though it was small there, we had a maid, Anna. Having a maid was a sign of being middleclass. One had to go shopping for fresh food each day, because there was no such thing as a refrigerator. Later we had an "ice chest" for which we had to buy blocks of ice from a special vendor who came to the door. There were, of course, no washing machines, no dishwashers, no electrical household devices, except, I think, an electric iron later on. We also bought an electric vacuum cleaner after the war, which was considered a great luxury. So, it is understandable that my mother needed a maid. Also, practically, on the day when I was born, my parents got a home job, to make a little extra money, a job which they kept for the rest of their lives, and even I myself, while a student in Medical School, much later, did some of this work which paid quite well. It consisted in sorting prescriptions from various pharmacies, calculate the prices—all pharmacies had the same prices and there were not thousands of different medicines, but only one or two hundred. Then everything had to be added up on a hand-pulled calculating machine which made a lot of noise. I remember the sound of that machine when my parents worked late at night, after we had gone to bed. This way, my parents had a second income and they even enjoyed doing it. Beats cleaning windows, I guess! My father was a beginning chemist at the University Pharmacy. His plan was to get into research at the University. As a student he had been doing well and even got a prize for his doctoral thesis in chemistry. It seems that he had outgrown the dyslexia of his childhood.

Unfortunately, not much later, in 1938, after Hitler occupied Austria, my father lost his job at the University because he refused to join the Nazi party. Everybody who wanted to keep a good job had to join the party. A friend of his, a pharmacist, who had joined the Nazis and who owned a pharmacy, employed him, more or less as a slave laborer working long hours with a minimum wage. He usually came home very late. I hardly remember anything about him from my early childhood. The times were immensely difficult then. At the University there had been physical altercations between groups of students often provoked by some SA gangs. The SA were the famous "brownshirts," all fanatical Nazis, who later transferred into the "SS" (Hitler's Sturmscharen— storm troops), after Hitler had personally killed Georg Strasser, the leader of the SA, and many other SA men. These young men, both the SA and the later SS, consisted of disenchanted, poorly educated young men from the lowest classes, often were criminals, who loved physical violence. They were the ones who had vandalized Jewish stores in Germany and later in Austria too, harassed Jewish people wherever they found them, made them brush the sidewalks with toothbrushes and even injured Jewish children.

At the same time, they felt superior because Hitler had told them that Aryans were superior people, and the reason why Germany had to suffer so much after the First World War were the Jews, worse, that it had been the Jews who had conspired with the capitalist countries to make Germany surrender, and even worse that the Jews were contriving for dominance of the entire world. My father belonged to a Catholic Student Organization (Kartellverband) which consisted of male students who were interested in lifelong "Brotherhood," social get-togethers with a lot of beer drinking and with a chance to get help by their older fraternity brothers. For many students from the smaller towns this was a Godsend because they were often invited by their older members to Sunday dinners, where they got to know the daughters of these older members and often married them. They had special formal dances during each Carnival season in the Emperor's palace, very elegant, all the girls in white long ballgowns, and the students in black dress suits. My mother had met my father in one of these dances. There were also fraternities for the non-Catholic, arch conservative students who tended toward the Nazi party. Some of these fraternities had the tradition of dagger fencing, not for athletic reasons, but for revenge or purely for tradition's sake. Many of these students ended up with scars in their faces from fencing for the rest of their lives. There were also fraternities who called themselves "Singers" with or without dagger fencing. They were often from old, traditional, aristocratic, military families. They all became Nazis first in Germany, later after the "Anschluss" in Austria too. There were also Socialist, Communist, Jewish student organizations. The Austrian Socialists, both before the First World War and after, had been successful in introducing adult education, outlawing child labor, and introducing social legislation. Unfortunately, there was a Civil War in Austria in the 1920s, stirred by the Sowjet Communists, between the socialists and the Christian Democrats (who were neither very Christian nor democratic). The Socialists lost and hundreds of them were hanged in the Central Prison of Vienna. After that disaster, the road was cleared for the Fascists in Austria to become stronger and have a Fascist as an Austrian chancellor (Dollfuss), who nevertheless was later assassinated by more fanatical Fascists. At that time in history, the road was wide open for Adolf Hitler, who invaded Austria with his well-equipped German Army. Austria had practically no functioning army and could not have stopped the Germans for even one hour. It was probably a wise decision not to fight the Germans, tens of thousands of young people would have lost their lives. Still, during the night, after Hitler had arrived in Vienna and given his famous or infamous speech at the "Heldenplatz" (Heroes' Place) in the center of Vienna, some 8000 Austrian patriots and intellectuals were grabbed by the German Gestapo (Secret Police) and sent to concentration camps, mostly to Mauthausen in Austria or Dachau in Bavaria. Many of them never came back and those who did had learned their lesson. They were sitting in the same prison cells with their former enemies from the Civil War and had to get along. After the war, they formed the new Austrian government consisting of a coalition between Socialists and Christian Democrats which is holding up until today.

Needless to say, my parents went through difficult times. The earliest memory I have of myself and my Mutti is me lying on a couch, fairly content, with my safety blanket and drinking sweet, warm milk from a bottle. We must have still lived at Steingasse and I was probably one or two years old. For some reason, I wanted my Mutti to come over which she refused. My younger sister Elfi was a baby then, if she even had been born then. I was told that I learned how to walk in the nearby "Belvedere Garden," the park, where the famous Prince Eugen of Savoy had his palace built by the Habsburg Emperors as a sign of her gratitude for his having driven the Turks out of the Habsburg Monarchy. I cannot image a more beautiful place for a child to learn how to walk—even though I do not remember the palace. My sister Elfi was a sickly child suffering from an inner ear infection, contracted, my parents kept saying, in the hospital after she was born, when the midwife placed her on a cold, drafty windowsill. "Survival of the Fittest!" I, on the other hand, must have been a handful, always in motion, always curious. At one point, I was told, Mutti was ready to throw me out of the window of the third floor. I was a well-fed, strong baby, whereas my sister was more dainty at that time. This changed completely ten years later.

Welzel 1939

Soon, after the Anschluss (Austria's occupation by the Germans) we moved into a large apartment in my grandparents' house. This apartment had been rented by a Jewish family. The Gestapo came one day and picked them up and took them to Theresienstadt, a concentration camp in Czechoslovakia. Most inmates were later transported to Auschwitz. Nobody ever came back, at least nobody whom we had known. There was nothing my grandparents could have done to save this Jewish family—one could even be sent to a concentration camp just for giving food to a Jewish family. Supposedly, the Jewish lady put a "hex" on this apartment when the Gestapo dragged her out. It seems that this curse was effective. In 1940, my father was recruited into the German Army, completely against his will and in spite of him being older than other recruits and having a family with two children. He was sent to Stalingrad, spent five years in Russian and Siberian prison camps (he wrote his Memoirs about those years). This apartment house was partially bombed, and my grandparents had to have it repaired at their cost. While we were away from Vienna, in 1945, some non-paying renters were placed into our apartment who had probably been bombed out, but it took us a long time to get them out. Then, the curse continued. In 1953, after my father finally got a good position as the chief of a huge hospital pharmacy in Lainz, the largest pharmacy in Europe, supplying 4000 beds, we moved into that hospital, into a so-called apartment for live-in professionals. My Mutti's brother Hans established his medical practice in our old apartment, but at the age of 64 he died of cancer of the stomach, whereas his only son died of AIDS in 1982, one of the first AIDS patients to die in Vienna. He had been a talented musician who had even composed a Mass, and then his mother, my Aunt Poldi, slowly developed Alzheimer's disease and died after long suffering.

The curious story of Frau Windhager (Mrs. Windhager), our neighbor. She was in her 80s when she lived right next door to us in a tiny studio without kitchen or bath. She died in 1941 or 1942 of a stroke. I happened to be outside in the corridor, when I saw her carried out on a stretcher. I saw her look at me with very tired eyes. We all knew that she was dying and felt an enormous loss. One or two days later, I saw a tall man in a black uniform with high black boots, an SS man apparently, enter her apartment. He was her son whom she had never told me about. I had never seen him before, it seems that he had never visited his mother, but now he took all her belongings out of her apartment, including her Last Will. At least that is what my mother told me later. I did not know it at that time, but Mutti told us later that Frau Windhager had told her that my sister and I should be the heirs to her jewelry collection. My Mutti was wise enough not to mention anything about the Last Will, it was better for us to let him steal everything than for us to end up in a concentration camp. It was the custom at that time, as in all dictatorships, for the men in power to dispose of their opponents or all unwanted persons by declaring them to be "Enemies of the State." With our family history of being "politically unreliable," I am glad that Mutti was clever enough to let him have the jewelry. How come a simple woman like Frau Windhager even owned valuable jewelry? This is her story: She had been the personal maid of the Duchess of Metternich for most of her life. The only salary she ever got were occasional pieces of jewelry. In the course of so many years of service she must have assembled a nice collection of valuable jewelry, which was her great pride. When the Duchess died she retired with a small dowry from the Duchess, in order to get married. In the 19th century, a girl had to bring a dowry into marriage, or she could not get married. She often told my Mutti about her years with the Duchess. She said that the dogs were better treated by aristocrats than their servants. It was part of her job to accompany the Duchess on all her travels and wear the key to the jewelry box around her neck. She also had to stay up every night when the Duchess was out at a party or some function until she returned which was sometimes as late as 3 A.M. Then she had to brush her hair with one hundred strokes with a special brush, which supposedly kept the hair of the aristocratic ladies silky. She had to take her meals near the Duchess at a separate table. This is how she learned to eat so daintily which we always admired. She said that the Duchess trained her how to eat by forcing her to hold a book between her elbows and her chest. She was also in charge of the Duchess' wardrobe, which she had to keep well maintained, the furs had to be winterized and of course everything had to be spick and span at all times. Aristocratic ladies were in the habit of travelling a lot, they were the only people who could afford to travel frequently for fun only. Frau Windhager had to travel with the Duchess while taking care of her travel wardrobe and doing all the odds and ends that a travelling Duchess needs. So she ended up seeing a lot of the world, but with the eyes of a servant ranked lower than the dogs. She probably told Mutti much more, but we were not privy to all the details. One of her stories comes to mind: Once while travelling on a boat in Italy she saw a person attacked and devoured by a shark; after that she was always afraid of swimming. The Duke of Metternich had been an important person within the Austro-Hungarian Monarchy. He negotiated the redistribution of land in Europe at the famous Congress of Vienna in the year 1815, after the defeat of Napoleon. He also established a Police State in the first half of the 19th century in the Habsburg Empire in order to prevent another Revolution like the French Revolution. History tells that it was rather grim living at that time and people had to be very careful what they said aloud—History has a tendency to repeat itself! The Duke was quite old when he married the very young Duchess who survived him by many years. The Duchess herself was quite elderly when she employed this very young girl from the country as her personal maid, perhaps around 1880. This means that Frau Windhager may have been born in the 1860s and died in the 1940s at the age of over 80 years old, which makes sense. After retiring from her service, Frau Windhager married a Mr. Windhager and they had one son. Mr. Windhager turned out to be an alcoholic and treated her so badly that she ran away from him. At that time there was not such a thing as an old age pension, so Mrs. Windhager, totally impoverished, had to make a living by sewing for other people. She said that she never sold any of her jewelry. My Mutti first engaged her to do some sewing in our household, but soon she graduated to be more like our gouvernante and my Mutti's companion. Her only son became an antisocial person and under Hitler joined the SS, and to my knowledge, she lost all contact with him. I still wonder sometimes how many people this SS man had killed during the war, what he did with the precious jewelry stolen from us children, and if he too denied ever having been a member of the Nazi party, like so many others.

It seems that my Oma got along well with her Jewish customers. When the Nazis started harassing Jews and taking all their possessions and forbidding them to enter non-Jewish shops—they had already taken all the Jewish shops away and the Jewish people had no place to buy food or other necessities. I heard rumors that some Jewish families had trusted my Oma and that she helped them secretly. I was about five years old, when I was visiting with my Oma and there was a knock at the door. She opened it furtively and would not let me take a really good look, but I did get a glimpse of an old man with a little girl of the same age as I was, poorly dressed, looking like beggars. I saw my Oma put some hot soup and a pot of some other food with bread take outside her entry door and place it on the window in the corridor, very carefully, making sure that nobody else had seen them. It was dangerous to help Jews. The least that happened to people who did that was a good beating by the SA gangs. But I heard also that some people were taken to concentration camps for doing this. I heard much later that one Jewish lady had taken a trunkful of embroideries to my Oma's shop for safekeeping, just before they were transported away and never seen again.

My father could have "aryanized" a Jewish pharmacy, as many of his colleagues did, but he refused to join the Nazis and was simply too decent to steal Jewish property. If he had done so, he could have stayed at home during the war (instead of spending it in Russia) and after the war, these pharmacies were never returned. To whom? Nobody came back from Auschwitz. My mother had more ambivalent feelings about Jews in Vienna. My mother had spent, as I mentioned already, her childhood in Styria (Steiermark) with her grandparents. When she came back to Vienna, she spoke the local dialect from her village in Steiermark. She thinks that the children in her public school, many of whom were Jewish, made fun of her dialect. Also that some Jewish children gave opera tickets and other gifts to the teachers. Her parents then sent her to a private Catholic school where she was thoroughly indoctrinated in traditional Catholicism. When she graduated from her teachers' training college, she could not find a job due to the enormous unemployment in Germany and Austria. The only job that she could find was privately tutoring a child in a Jewish family. She said that she liked the job, but the family treated her as if she were a servant. Once she brought some of her own children's books to that child, but the Jewish mother refused to accept them because they were old and "unclean." I think that my mother felt deeply insulted and since that has never liked Jews. Like most other people in Nazi occupied Europe she did not know what was really happening to the disappeared Jews, until she learned the truth. It must have been in 1943—we lived in my uncle's house in Steiermark—I must have been seven years old, when I overheard a whispered conversation between my mother and my Oma who was visiting from Vienna. I pretended to sleep, but I remember every word that was said. My Oma had a cousin who had been a missionary with the order of the Salesians in Brazil. He had been sent back to Vienna because of illness. It is well known that the Vatican knew what was happening to the Jews—and so did my relative, the priest. He had told my Oma about the gas chambers in the Polish concentration camps. It seems that many countries in America knew about the crimes of the concentration camps. It was only in the German-occupied countries, where truly most people had no idea, because of the propaganda and because one would be executed if one was caught listening to a foreign radio station. How did the Vatican know? Today we regard Pope Pius XII as a Fascist who even contributed to the Holocaust. There were, however, many decent and even saintly priests, monks and nuns who helped many Jews by accepting them into their monasteries to hide them there, and a few had even been in concentration camps and had been able, mysteriously, to escape. They told the Pope about these crimes, but it seems that the Pope did nothing until the very end.

We were still in Vienna, in my second grade of elementary school, when my mother, my sister, and Eri, a girlfriend, took a stroll in a nearby park where once there had been a Jewish cemetery. In the recent past this cemetery had been completely vandalized, desecrated, and the bones and skulls were lying around in the mud. My girlfriend lifted one skull on top of a stick and marched around sing-songing, "This is a Jewish head, and they are all dead." My mother immediately dragged us out of the park and forbade us to ever go back and play there. But again, every word was in a hush-hush voice, nobody was supposed to know anything, everybody was afraid. The fact is that I really never played there again, and I thought that it had been pretty gross of Eri to play with bones.

My Mother And The Jews

Most Catholics had, until the second Vatican Council in the early 1960s, very ambivalent feelings toward the Jews. The priests had preached from the pulpits for centuries that the Jews had "murdered" Jesus and are therefore responsible for this for eternity. They never mentioned that Mary was a Jewish girl and that Jesus spoke Aramaic, the most common language at that time in the Middle East, derived from Hebrew. We all know about bloody, horrific persecutions, the crimes of the Inquisition, the programs, and the Holocaust. We all know that Jews were not allowed to own land, join the Armed Forces, or go into certain forms of profession, until Emperor Franz Josef in the 19th century issued a law which permitted Jews to go into all professions, or join the army. This is why so many Jewish people came to Vienna from all over the Monarchy, and soon became very successful due to their tradition of studying hard and teaching their children early on to have respect for learning. The Christians in the Austro-Hungarian Monarchy who were not so successful blamed the Jews of having better connections, using deceitful business practices, lying in Court, extorting high interest rates from their debtors, etc. Sigmund Freud's family too had come to Vienna from Moravia, at that time. His family was poor and so Dr, Freud had to become a general practitioner instead of a research scientist. Thanks to God, that he specialized in diseases of the nerves and the mind, and the rest is history.

Forward ten years later—I was an exchange student in Erie, Pennsylvania, at the age of 16 years, where I saw for the first time in my life Jewish people without the star of David on their black coats. As a result of a newspaper article that had been written about me and the exchange program, a Jewish girl from Budapest contacted me. She and her family had miraculously survived the war in Hungary, because they pretended to be Aryans, with their mother having blonde hair and blue eyes. After the war they were able to emigrate to the USA. I was happy to find almost a countryman and Daisy and I became good friends. Upon my return to Vienna, I visited some of Daisy's friends and we invited each other to our homes. I noticed that my mother was not very friendly and again I knew that my mother really did not like Jews.

Forward another three years. I was a beginning medical student and was excited about meeting so many different nationalities at the Medical School. Austria, being a poor country at that time, gave its part of aid to third-world countries in the form of education. Hundreds of students were accepted from the Arabic world, from India, from Africa, etc., for almost zero tuition and got an excellent education there. I quickly found some Egyptian and Iranian friends, all from good families, and felt flattered and happy to have found such good friends. I even had a little romance with Anwar from Alexandria whose mother was Viennese and therefore he could live with his grandparents. He is still alive as a general practitioner near Vienna. One of the Israeli students—Israelis and Arabic students got along quite well at the University—was Paul Rudich. His father had been a doctor in Vienna and therefore Paul spoke fluent German. He had been an officer in the Israeli Airforce before he could go to Vienna to study Medicine. He was much more mature than I, needless to say. He told me that his father had been very much liked by his patients, one of whom had become an SS man after Hitler's takeover of Austria. It was this SS man who alerted Dr. Rudich of the imminent danger hours before they were supposed to be picked up by the Gestapo, he even helped the family to take a train to Italy. Finally they ended up in Israel where his father started a practice in Tell Aviv. Paul was a child when Israel fought its first war with the Arabic countries surrounding Israel and he was employed to carry ammunition and guns to the front. I learned so much from him, such as more responsibility, total honesty and decency in even the smallest things of daily life. My mother was horrified when she found out that I was keeping company with a Jew.

In the beginning of the first semester, I was knocked down by a motorcycle in the street and broke the radius of my right arm, which I did not even notice at once, until the pain came. Paul had somehow seen this and took me immediately to the emergency room for treatment and then he took me to his home because I was not ready for the long ride on public transportation. There we called my mother and asked her to pick me up with her car. She was appalled that I was in a Jewish man's room—I guess she would have been less angry if I had called her from Hell—the fact that I was injured counted nothing in comparison to being in a Jew's home. So much for religion! She suspected that he was my boyfriend and that I might possibly get stuck with a Jewish man. This made her physically ill and emotionally out of control. She said that he would never be accepted into our family, but that I too would never be accepted by his family. Everybody in Vienna was supposed to know that Jewish boys would rape their Catholic servant girls, but never marry them. Possibly Adolf Hitler's father was the result of such a liaison when his grandmother had worked as a maid for a Jewish family in Vienna. She and my grandmother had Masses read in order for me to get rid of this Jewish liaison and my grandmother prayed a "Nine-day prayer" (Novene) for me. Another thing happened: Slowly I noticed that I was no longer invited by my Austrian colleagues to go to parties, dances, picnics, etc. I had not counted on Austrian Xenophobia, and that did not just concern the Israelis. Every girl who dated an Arabic, or God forbid, an African student, was totally shunned. The fact that the Neo-Nazis, of whom there were many, called them "whores," I fortunately never found out. In spite of all this, I would have stuck to my friend Paul, but life had different plans for me.

Back to our apartment in the 18th district, at Anastasius Gruengasse 3, into which we moved, when I was about four years old, in the year 1940 or 1941. This was the apartment where a Jewish family had lived. The apartment building belonged to my grandparents. Most of the 18th district was an upper-middle-class district with many beautiful mansions which belonged to aristocrats or rich Jewish or Non-Jewish families. We used to admire these houses with their well-kept gardens when we went on our Sunday afternoon walks to a large park with a name reminding people of the Turkish sieges of Vienna, "Tuerkenschanzpark" ("Fortress against the Turks"). The Jewish houses had by then been taken away from them in the so-called "Aryanization" program, and the non-Jewish homes belonged to upper-middle-class families, many of whom had become Nazis. The homes which had been "aryanized" were occupied by important members of the Austrian and German Nazi party. In my first year of elementary school already I found myself surrounded by the daughters of famous Nazis, such as my neighbor, Susi Kaltenbrunner, whose father later was hanged at the Nuremberg trial for his war crimes. After the war, most of these Nazi families could stay in their stolen homes because hardly anybody ever came back from Auschwitz. So even later, in high school, I found myself surrounded by fanaticized Nazi daughters. More about that later.

Our apartment consisted of one living room, a dining salon, one bedroom, where the whole family slept, one entrance hall with a toilet inside, which was a luxury, because most people had to use a common toilet outside in the corridor. And Luxury upon luxury, we had a bathroom and a maid's room which was entered from the corridor. All these rooms except for the living room were never heated, partially because coal was rationed and it would have been too expensive to have a stove in each room. The poor maid had to live and sleep in the kitchen which was slightly warmer from the gas stove.

Those "maids" were young girls who had finished secondary school at the age of 14 years. Girls who had finished high school did not have to work as maids, they were encouraged to go for higher education, because Hitler needed all the professional men in his wars and expected the women to become doctors and engineers. Hitler had ordered that every "German" had to give his/her best to the "Thousand-Year Empire" to be established by him. Unmarried, lower-educated girls had to move in with families in order to help the "German Mother" who was supposed to have at least four children "for the Leader." In reality, many of these girls also had to function as spies on their families, observe all anti-German behavior or words spoken and report everything to the Gestapo. Many of them had been fanatically indoctrinated in Nazi ideology and possibly regarded it as their duty to support the "Thousand-Year Empire." So all families would only communicate with each other in whisper tones or not at all. We children were always told by my mother, to never, ever tell anybody in school what was spoken at home, although I don't even remember that my parents spoke openly about their feelings, at least not in the presence of us or the maid. Whenever the "Fuehrer" gave a speech, all the people would turn on their radios very loud and open the windows in order to make it known that they were listening and appreciating Hitler's words. This is similar in all dictatorships, particularly in the Sowjet Union. About the maids, most of them probably never reported anything, because they themselves came from families whose father had been recruited into the German Army against their wishes. And most were rather poor. Their wages were paid by the Government, but were very low. Also 14-year-old girls are not much help to young mothers and had to be taught all the household duties.

We had one Nazi family in our apartment building, our next-door neighbors. Since they were good Nazis, Mr. Waldhausl was never drafted into the army and could stay at home throughout the War. They had one daughter, Lise, of my age. She was always fat in contrast to most other people who were beginning to have less food in those years. We received food stamps according to the work that people performed. It was a crime to be dishonest with food stamps. As the war progressed, most people received the equivalent of 900 calories daily in the form of fat-free milk, potatoes, some vegetables, meat very rarely, bread and flour, very little sugar, some seasonal fruit. Somehow, my mother and we children never suffered of hunger—we are all small eaters; my mother even gave some of her food stamps to a family with growing boys. By the way, Mr. Waldhausl's swastika badge, the sign of being a member of the Nazi party, disappeared when the Russian Army arrived in Vienna. Like millions of others, he denied ever having been a member of the party.

My father, my sister and I, 1941

A few days before I began my first year of elementary school, in 1942, my father, who happened to be on furlough from the Army, took me aside. He told me in a sad voice that he would have to leave the next morning for Russia, probably for a very long time. He even added that he might never come back because so many soldiers were killed in the war. I remember every word of this conversation to this day. The concept of death was not in my brain yet, I had never seen a dead person. At my age, not even six years old, I had been seeing very little of my father, because he had already been drafted into the German Army, needless to say, totally against his wish. Before that, he had been working such long hours as a pharmacist and even on weekends, that I hardly knew him. I understood that it would be horrible for him to be in Russia where I knew it gets extremely cold in the winters. On the other hand, I knew I would not miss him much because we were already spending most of the time without him. As I grew older and began understanding things better, and he was still far away and possibly dead, I felt millions of regrets for knowing that I would not miss him very much at that time.

About school: In some bizarre way, I profited from the Nazi ideology. Because my father had a Ph.D. and my mother was a trained teacher, I was considered to be "genetically" more intelligent according to Nazi pseudoscience. When I started school, I was automatically sent into the "A" train. There was also a "B" train for children from non-academic families and a "C" train for the slow learners. More severely retarded or handicapped children were euthanized by the Nazi doctors and so were all the mentally ill until the Catholic Church finally intervened and threatened to withdraw their cooperation with Hitler, something that Hitler could not afford because almost the entire population of Austria and Bavaria was Catholic. What this shows is that the Catholic Church had enough power even during Hitler's regime to stop the killing of thousands of people. Who knows, if the Church could not have prevented the killing of millions of Jews, gypsies, Slavic people, if the Pope had really shown his power and had never made a contract with Hitler. It seems that the fight against atheistic Communism was more important to the Pope than the lives of millions of innocent people!

Now an even more bizarre story in relation to the Nazi ideology. Unbeknown to me and my mother, I was lefthanded and dyslexic. Using my left hand for writing was strictly "verboten." I could even have been considered to be an abnormal child and we all know what happened to them. Dyslexia was not recognized at that time—my father had suffered severely from unrecognized dyslexia in his days of elementary school; my son Reinhard was also severely dyslexic, but in his case it was recognized and he got special help in the first grades and everybody just joked about it and he never lost his self-esteem. He even said as a little boy that he did not need to learn spelling correctly because he would have a secretary to do that for him. My two daughters, Monica and Daniela, were slightly dyslexic and went to some special classes for this. The "A" train in school experimented with a new teaching technique, a "Gestalt Method." I remember that I never learned the alphabet or spelling, but I was presented with a picture of an object together with the writing underneath, for instance, the drawing of a house with the written word underneath. In this way, I could imprint in my brain the symbol together with the written word. Our mothers had to promise in the beginning of the schoolyear to practice "reading" with us every afternoon. My mother later said that it had not been easy either for her nor for me to learn reading in this way. The advantage of this method was, that we progressed very quickly, and by the end of the first schoolyear, I was able to read just about any book. Had I been sent to a regular ABC school, my dyslexia would have become apparent and I might have become the "class idiot."

When my sister began school in 1943 things had become so disorganized with the bombing of the schools, changing schools every month, spending many nights in the "bomb shelters"—there was no more regular education. Those bomb shelters, by the way, were our own coal cellars in the under basement of the apartment buildings. Needless to say that any fire from a bomb would have burned the coal together with our bodies or if the waterpipes had been hit in a bomb attack all the water would have poured into this cellar and we would have all drowned. One of my uncles drowned this way in his mandatory bomb shelter. Was I afraid during those nights and the loud alarm sirens before an attack and after? My mother and the maid managed to awake us gently, pack us in warm blankets and carry us into the cellar without panic and with some of our dolls. One older boy played puppet theater with our dolls for us. Of course, nobody was allowed to show any fear or say anything about these attacks because we Germans were going to take terrible revenge against the British and we were all working for the huge "final victory" at the end.

I have been frequently asked if we had to join the "Hitler Youth" before we began school and later in the afternoons during our schoolyears. I was once invited by the Hitler girls where they served us chocolate and cake, something that had become unheard of outside. I begged my mother to send me to the Hitler girls where I expected chocolate and cake every day. She was very clever, however, and refused to send us to the Hitler Youth on the pretext that we were too fragile to withstand infectious illnesses. We were indeed both small, not because we were fragile, but because of genetics. Instead, she sent us to a kindergarten in a nearby Jesuit Church, the Church of St. Canisius. I remember that we both liked it there with a young priest playing ball or puppets with us, singing a lot of "holy" songs and also getting some character training, like postponing certain pleasures, not always looking around, when somebody entered the room which serves me to this day. At the same time we learned everything about our religion. By the time I entered high school (the 5th grade in an American school) I knew so much about the Old and New Testament, church history, the saints, that my teacher in Religion (Religion was and is a subject in Austrian schools) made me his assistant at the age of ten. I have always proudly regarded myself to be a student of the Jesuits.

In my second year of elementary school, in the year 1943, the air raids became so frequent that my mother decided to leave Vienna and move in with her mother's side of the family who lived in the East Steiermark, in the village of Tautendorf. Everybody in that village was family. It takes indeed a whole village to bring up a child. There were all the old aunts and uncles who could no longer work in the fields who watched us openly or behind their curtains. If anybody had got into trouble, there would have been help immediately. By the way, that part of Austria, Steiermark (Styria), had been an archdukedom within the Austro-Hungarian Monarchy for centuries and history says that the relationship between the Habsburg dukes and the population had always been a good one. These dukes were mostly benign, did not overtax the people, tried to establish a good educational system, and frequently visited their villages. There was even a love song for one of these dukes.

We ended up living in the small farm of my Uncle Franz on a little hill with a beautiful view of the other houses and the nearby village. His younger brother, Johann, had inherited the large family farm which was contrary to established customs. Uncle Franz had an alcohol problem and therefore his father did not give him the family farm which was huge with vineyards, horses, servants, several houses, almost like a small estate. Uncle Franz' house consisted of one large kitchen/living room with a huge woodstove in which my Aunt Lina baked the most delicious bread each week, but it also served as the only heater for the entire house. I can still taste this homemade, freshly baked, flavorful, warm bread! With butter it was more delicious than anything else I have ever eaten. There was one bedroom for my aunt and uncle which was so cold in the winter that they could keep the milk fresh in there. We got the little extra room which was tiny, but at that time it was sufficient for us. We had left Vienna only with our suitcases, and so we did not need a lot of space for our wardrobes. My mother knew some families in Vienna who refused to leave their spacious, elegant apartments and their furs and clothes behind, only to be bombed out and losing everything, even sometimes their lives. Actually, owning almost nothing, but having a huge family in a beautiful place, lots of animals and friends in the village ended up becoming the paradise of my childhood. I am almost ashamed to say that these years were the happiest years of my life, when so many other children were killed in the war, not to mention the poor Jewish children in the concentration camps! When I visited this village 60 years later I realized how tiny everything had been there. Today, the great grandchildren of Uncle Franz and Aunt Lina are using the old house only for storage and office space for their thriving business with fruit juices and honey. Other farmers in that village specialized in lean, grass-fed pigs or poultry in the 1990s and probably still do so and are doing very well.

I adored my Uncle Franz when we lived in his house. He was always very kind to us children and allowed us to use the upper floor of a barn to play "house" with the village children. Since we had some dolls and teddy bears from Vienna, we soon became quite popular and every child wanted to play in our "house." Uncle Franz even got us some old furniture for our "house." We children did not realize that we neither owned anything nor could we buy anything in the empty stores in the larger village nearby. We drank wonderful fresh milk from my uncle's cows, ate whatever the vegetable garden produced, ate the homemade bread, and sometimes even got a little bit of homemade ham or sausages. Directly opposite of our small room was the pigsty. I don't remember any bad odors, because my aunt kept the pigs very clean. Each morning, my aunt would go into the pigsty to feed them with leftovers from the kitchen and they would squeak in all imaginable melodies. Each pig had a name and a personality and so did the cows. Baby pigs are the cutest animals and the older ones were very smart. Unfortunately, each winter one of these pigs was slaughtered to provide the family with ham which was smoked in the chimney, and with lard. My sister and I were not allowed to watch the slaughtering, but could hear them cry with terror and scream like human beings. Once I watched one of my favorite baby calves pulled away from her mother to be dragged to the butcher. I asked where they were taking this beautiful calf and my aunt said that it would be butchered so that we could eat tasty veal. I cried and tried to rescue this baby and promised never in my life to eat meat again, but was not successful. For many days I could hear the calf's mother howl and cry for her lost baby. I soon found out that even there was a political undertone. "German" farmers were forced to deliver a certain portion of their animals and farm products to the Nazi government, to feed the populations in the cities and the Military, of course. I understood that they were not supposed to do their own butchering or wine or Schnapps making. There was a "commissar" in each village whose job was to make sure that the farmers obeyed the laws. In our village, this Nazi overseer was a friend of the family. Whenever there was an illegal butchering he was invited to the feast and returned home with enough meat for his family for the rest of the year. I am sure that at the end of the war, the farmers of the village protected him from capture by the Russians.

My uncle also had several tall, fat, large cows who produced so much milk that my uncle won a prize for having the best cows in the entire district. At the same time, these cows were his only source of energy. There were no agricultural motors, hardly electricity—we used petroleum lamps later in the war—no tractors, no trucks—we lived practically at the tail end of the Middle Ages. These cows had to work hard. They pulled the ploughs in the fields and the heavy wooden wagons which was the only form of transportation. My aunt milked the cows twice each day by hand. This milk was so rich that my mother sometimes pulled inches of milkfat from the top of the milk containers, from which she made us whipped cream. At that time farmers did not use any fertilizers or pesticides, instead, the dirty straw underneath the cows was spread out in the fields together with the products of the outdoor toilet, a rather smelly business, but we all ended up eating 100% organic food, no sugar (which was not available in the stores) and even the commonly used and beloved cider ("Most") was homemade from apples. "Schnapps" was made from prunes in late fall. There was little illness in that village except for men who drank too much alcohol. The older people did develop cataracts and became blind, or osteoarthritis which was common possibly as a result of a lifelong of very hard work in the fields and with the animals. Because so many of the young men had been drafted into the German Army, this hard work was mostly done by women and some Russian prisoners of war who had supposedly volunteered to help out in German farms. My Uncle Hans had one tall, nice-looking Russian who could not speak one word of German. Even if he had, he would not have understood the local dialect. Of course, we children had to do our portion of household and farm duties too. When we went to our friends to play with them, we usually had to help them finish their chores first before they were allowed to play.

One day, my Uncle Franz took me aside and asked me if I could help him graze the cows. He suggested that my sister and I lead the cows on a rope into the pastures along the roads and walkways where they would find rich, tasty clover. Most of this land was public land and the cows were not allowed to roam about unsupervised. Initially, I was a little afraid of these huge cows, they could have killed a child with one kick of their hooves. But Mimi, Mona, Kati, and Lisa were only interested in the lush, fat grass and rather than I leading them, they would lead me to the richest places which they ate bare and then moved on to the next rich place. After a while, we were allowed to take the cows to a large meadow to which many other children would bring their cows for grazing. While the cows were feeding, we children would have ourselves a party by frying potatoes on a fire. I have never eaten potatoes that good! These summer evenings remain in my memory as perfect, wondrous, and adventurous. We were in the Garden of Eden. One evening, a boy, somewhat older than I, joined us from a neighboring village. He would entertain us with his stories of his heroic deeds and gossip, we would listen to him with fascination. Later at home, I heard my aunt say something not nice about this boy, upon which my mother no longer allowed us to join the village children on that pasture. I missed his stories. So soon I began writing my own stories. Books were not available in those years, the libraries and bookstores were empty (people had to use the paper from books for kindling). In school too, there were no books; the teachers had to write everything on a blackboard and we children had to copy from those blackboards. We did have some small notebooks and pencils and some even had fountainpens. I filled several notebooks with stories of witches, kings, princesses, heroes, and speaking animals on our kitchen table which was mine after school because the farmers were out in the fields. In the winter, the kitchen stove radiated cozy warmth. Our housedog "Prinzi," some kind of a mut, with a large head, short legs, could have won a prize for being one of the ten ugliest dogs in all of Germany. He and the cats, of whom there so many that nobody ever counted them spent magic afternoons in that kitchen. In those years, we never received any mail from my father in Russia. We had no newspapers either; my uncle refused to buy Nazi propaganda, there was not even a radio in the house, so I was literally ignorant of what was going on in the outside world. In school we were taught that the German Army was relentlessly successful and victorious. I was certain that my father would come home from the war, but once I overheard my mother cry in bed and I thought it was because we had not heard from Papa for such a long time. I overheard some gossiping by older women that Stalingrad had fallen into the hands of the Russians and that the Red Army was moving westwards towards us. Whereas the German Army was also moving toward the west in full retreat from the Red Army.

It was in early 1943 when we had moved to Steiermark. I was in my second year of grade school. There was a grade school in Soechau, a small town within walking distance from Tautendorf, which was also the only place where they had some stores, a pretty baroque church, and a few country inns, bars for the locals for drinking. School in Soechau turned out to be exhaustingly boring because the other second graders could not yet read. So the class had to repeat the same text over and over in an attempt to teach the children how to read. My mother could have placed me into a higher grade of that school, but again there was a political reason why she did not do that. In the upper classes, the children were taught incessantly about the wonderful leaders of the Hitler Empire, and efforts were made to recruit them into the Hitler Youth. My sister was in first grade and barely learned how to spell the alphabet, but at least she was less bored. My classmates soon became aware that I did not quite belong into their class. Soon after our arrival, as I walked home from school, I was suddenly confronted by a gang of local boys and girls who started chiding me, throwing stones at me, and calling me things like "haughty city wench," "You think you are better than we are!" and even beat me up a bit. To this day, I have no idea who these children had been. I had never consciously seen these children before and would not have recognized them later because, unbeknown to me, I was already nearsighted. When I arrived at home, quite shaken up, I told my uncle, Mutti, and everybody else what had happened. Mutti said that she was going to tell "Hansi," who was her cousin, but since he was the youngest child in a large family, he turned out to be only a few years older than I, but still he was my uncle. He was a sort of a village leader among the boys, strongly built, used to hard work at his age already, and often quite funny. I remember that he showed up and made me tell him exactly what these children had looked like, what exactly they had done to me, and then he said he knew who they were and that he would get even with them. Whatever he did or not did, from that day on there were not even the slightest altercations with any village children. On the contrary, all the children from the neighbor houses became quite protective of me and my sister and picked us up every morning for school. From then on, I never had to walk alone any more and the 40-minute walk to school became quite enjoyable. Depending on the weather on the dirt road or along the railroad trails connecting our area with the capital of Steiermark, Graz. This was legally forbidden, but everybody had to do it. After some rainy days, the dirt roads were transformed into mud in which one could get stuck. The locals usually walked in the mud with bare feet carrying their shoes in a bundle only to put them on when they arrived in Soechau, where some of the roads were asphalt roads.

As the war progressed we experienced more and more shortages of everything, even paper, sewing material, fabric, etc. We were lucky because we produced practically everything that we needed on the farm. On weekends, my Aunt Lina spent a lot of time trying to catch a chicken—they fluttered remarkably quickly and noisily all over the stables and inside the house. Once caught, she must have decapitated them, because I watched the "dead" chickens run around without a head and fluttering their wings until they collapsed. The breaded and lard-baked chicken meat was delicious, but I usually had little appetite to eat them after watching their unsavory deaths. We also had rabbits in wooden stalls and could play with them whenever we wanted. They also disappeared one after another and reappeared in breaded form on the kitchen table after Sunday church. A funny story about our beloved, ugly dog Prinzi. I observed him once within a group of male dogs surrounding a female dog whom I did not know. Each male dog tried to copulate with the female dog until it was Prinzi's turn. His legs were short and the female dog was rather tall. So his attempts were unsuccessful and he walked home sadly. One day, my Uncle Franz brought home the loveliest, white goat baby. We were allowed to treat her as a pet, but she was not meant to be a pet, she was meant to become food. After she had gained some weight, my uncle sat down next to me and explained that he had to slaughter her and I should not be shocked if I hear her cry, and indeed she cried like a baby for quite a while. I thought that it had been very decent of him to tell me in advance and also he told me that this animal had been bought for consumption because food was getting sparser even on farms. I will never blame him for killing this lovely animal, but I lost my appetite to ever eat meat again.

We heard of more and more bomb attacks on all German and Austrian cities and even on small towns like Graz, where one of my uncles died in such an attack. Otherwise my family was lucky, all the men eventually came back from the war. One day, as I was walking home from school, I heard a plane flying very low. I instinctively ran down into the bed of a tiny creek and lay flat down in the water where

I felt secure. I had the feeling that this pilot could and would have shot at me if I had not hidden from him.

Soon, even in our little village, there were more and more days when we were told not to go to school. I was then in my third grade and had a big crush on my young, blonde, pretty teacher. Her last name was Hess. She allowed me to carry the pupils' homework and sometimes, even to help her correct them. Once she invited me to her home to have lunch with her and her mother. I was in heaven. One day, I overheard my mother ask her if she was, by any chance, a relative of the famous Rudolf Hess, a former friend of Hitler, a pilot, who had flown to England in 1941 or 1942, in order to negotiate a separate peace between England and Germany. All this is history now. It turned out that she was the sister of Rudolf Hess, which did not impress me very much, because I did not know about him at that time. I often thought about her later, after the war was lost, and so many former members of the circle around Hitler had either committed suicide or had been taken to the Trials in Nuremberg, or worse, were dragged by the Red Army to Russia.

In April 1945 we heard on a radio that the Red Army was approaching very fast into Germany and was engaged in heavy, bloody fights with the German Weapons SS in Hungary. One day I saw a line of heavy trucks stop at the house of my Uncle Hans. His house was the largest house in the village and so the Weapons SS made it into their headquarters, in order to defend the border against the approaching Red Army. At that time, as I learned later, the German Army no longer existed, partially all soldiers had been killed or had capitulated. Every man available, even 16-year-old boys, were incorporated into the Weapons SS. They had never, to my knowledge, participated in the crimes of the regular SS, but were the best trained fighters, but even they had some fanatics as I will prove shortly.

These were days of great confusion, and what was even worse, nobody knew what was really going on. The newspapers had always told lies, as they do in every dictatorship, and nobody believes the newspapers or the news on the radios. Soon we heard battle sounds day and night. The Russians had this huge machinegun, the so-called "Stalinorgan," which produced the most apocalyptic roars, twenty perhaps in one explosion, then silence for a few seconds, then another explosion and so on all night long. Echoing these roars were the German machineguns which were more like gunshots, but in rapid succession. The battlefield was only some thirty miles away from our village. Daily I saw German trucks filled with dead or wounded soldiers driving them to the nearest hospital in Furstenfeld, a small town, about one half-hour's train ride from Soechau. Most of the SS soldiers slept in the stables and warmed themselves next to outdoor wood fires where they also cooked their meager meals. I never heard that they stole food or livestock from the local farmers. My Uncle Hans had one Polish forced-labor maid and one Russian prisoner of war, to help on the farm. Both were very good people, kind to us children, and as I heard from my uncle very much afraid of the arriving Russian Army. We know from history that captured Russian soldiers, particularly those who had voluntarily helped in the German Industry, were sent to the Gulags of Siberia upon their arrival in Russia. Or they were immediately shot. Whatever happened to the Polish lady who was very young, nobody knew, but certainly not much good. Among these Weapons SS Troops were some younger officers who were good looking and very friendly toward us children. One of them came to my attention, because he said quite frankly that the war was lost and that so many young lives were unnecessarily sacrificed. I was told later that before the Russians arrived in our village, some fanatic had taken this officer out into the forest and had shot him. The whole village mourned for him. The roaring of the machineguns became louder and louder and the people were beginning to lose their nerves. Some prayed aloud and looked constantly at the sky because some old woman had said that she had seen a cross inside of a star. People were indeed hoping for some miracle to happen or even the second coming of Jesus Christ. I myself was afraid too, of course, but not for one moment did I think that we would not survive. I think that our Mutti instilled such a sense of security in us that we felt invulnerable. I will never forget a young SS officer motioning to us to come closer and to hold out our aprons, which we did hesitantly. Then he filled them with chocolates and candy with a big smile. This might have been his last ration and he knew that he would soon die or taken by the Russians who executed SS soldiers without discriminating between the Weapons SS and the criminal SS. This was the first chocolate after five years and the first candy after two or three years. May he have found a very special place in Heaven! We also saw endless wagon trains pulled by horses and loaded with German-speaking people from the Banat, a Germanic area in Romania. They were all fleeing from the Russians. These people were German farmers who had been sent three hundred years ago by the Austrian Emperors to repopulate those lands which had been devastated by the Turks, similar to Hungary after the Turks had been expelled. They wore strange, black clothes and spoke a German dialect which was hard to understand. They tried to tell us about the horrible things that the Russians had done to them and how they barely escaped leaving behind their beloved, well-kept farms and animals. These refugees never returned to their homelands and became "nationless" like millions of other refugees after the war. We would soon join this train of refugees.

Soon absolute panic spread. We expected the Red Army to arrive any hour now. The farmers dug holes into the ground in their fields to hide their bottles of Schnapps or whatever treasures they had. It was known that the Russians first demanded alcohol and then committed their atrocities when they were completely drunk. Many of these hiding places were never found after the Russian had left. Soon word came that all the women and children had to leave this area. Farmers who have to take care of their animals and fields can never flee in such a situation, they just have to survive somehow. Mutti, my sister and I did not have such responsibilities and were free to flee. But how? The troops had to flee too. So what my mother did was this: She bribed one of the SS truck drivers with a package of Havana cigars which she had been keeping for a special event and which were considered to be worth more than gold. This driver was to take us out of the battlefield. There was one problem, though, this truck was loaded with the bodies of dead SS soldiers. With our suitcases we jumped into the bed of this truck and made ourselves comfortable in between the dead soldiers. When the truck left our village, that was the only time when I cried. I felt so sorry for all the people left behind who, I was sure, would be killed by the Russians. Much later, when we returned, we found out that all the women had been raped, according to Stalin's personal order, and most of the animals had been consumed by the soldiers, the wonderful St. Bernard dog was shot by the Russians when he tried to defend his owner. Otherwise they occupied all the houses and the farmers had to hide in their orchards or vineyards. Thank God that it was May and the weather was warm enough to sleep outside. This did not last long because at the time of the total surrender of Germany, the Red Army was sent to occupy other areas of Austria. In the meantime we were stuck with the dead soldiers on the truck, all wrapped in grey blankets. I became curious and lifted a blanket a bit to see the soldier's face. To my astonishment I saw a boy not older than 15 or 16 years, I was nine at that time. This truck took us all the way to Graz, the capital of Steiermark. There we stayed with one of my grandmother's sisters who managed to get us on another truck the next day, together with another of my grandmother's sisters, Resi, her daughter Frieda and her little one-year-old son Erich. On that truck we spent a long time. It took us north into the mountains of Upper Steiermark into the valley of the Mur River, where nobody expected the Russians ever to get to. In Leoben, a small industrial town, we experienced an air raid so close by that I had the feeling that a bomb had just barely passed us by. Of course, the British or U.S. bomber planes would target a German SS truck! I did not even realize in what grave danger we had been. Finally we got into the mountains and it got considerably colder. The River Mur's name is an old Celtic name, like so many other places in those mountains have retained their Celtic or Pre-Celtic names, and the inhabitants of these valleys and mountains are the direct descendants of the first Bronze Age Europeans for about 4000 years. In one of the villages we had to get out of the truck and walk up the mountain into another village, where my Aunt Resi's husband had some distant relatives who owned large mountain farms there. They are all cow farmers because in those altitudes there is hardly any agriculture. So we arrived, early in the morning, like beggars and we were NOT welcome. The largest house belonged to three unmarried sisters, big, blonde, formidable looking in their long, local peasant dresses with aprons. Aunt Resi, Frieda and her baby were taken in hesitantly by these three Amazons, but my mother, my sister, and I were told to go to the neighbor's house. At that moment I really felt like a beggar, we were truly homeless! I was a bit surprised that nobody took pity on us even as we told them about the Russians. During wartime, it seems that people get bitter and compassionless, with only their own survival at heart. The next door neighbor did not have room for us either and sent us yet to another neighbor. Finally we found a small house with an attic filled entirely with old furniture belonging to another person. With great hesitation and accepting most of the money that my mother still owned, the owners of that house allowed us to live in the attic temporarily, but we were not allowed to use any of the furniture. Since everything had broken down by that time, my mother no longer received the small sum of money from the German government, which all the families of recruited soldiers were supposed to get. Since my father had never become an officer due to his political "unreliability," my mother received only something like 600 Mark as compared to officers' families who were paid more than 900 Mark, a sum that was sufficient to live comfortably on. Money had never been a conscious problem for me, because there was nothing to buy in the stores anyway. Then living on a farm, where my mother paid a small rent and contribution toward food, I was never aware that we had actually been poor throughout the war. Only now, living in that shabby stuffy attic filled with old furniture, I became aware that we were poor, disliked, unwelcome, unclean, and even hungry sometimes, and very hungry if my mother had not had extraordinary survival skills. She found a job carrying heavy buckets of milk from the neighbors' cows down the mountain into the larger village in the valley each morning. Probably a one-hour walk down the mountain trail and back up with the empty buckets. Sometimes she brought us a cup of heavy cream that she had secretly skimmed off the milk on which we feasted. She also got food from these farmers in the form of milk, bread, and some garden vegetables, and homemade cheese. Soon she discovered a restaurant in that larger village, Unzmarkt, was its name. And we began eating lunch there every day. The owner of the restaurant received some of the milk and pailfuls of raspberries from us children which we plucked right behind our house up the hill next to an ancient ruin which dated back into the 12th century. I noticed that this owner, an older gentleman, enjoyed seeing my mother and often sat with us at the table eating his lunch. At that time, there were only old men at home as civilians, because all the younger men, and, as I have already said, adolescent boys, had been recruited to defend the "Thousand-Year Empire" which by that time, only twelve years since Adolf Hitler's leadership had begun, no longer existed.

Regardless of the tragedies all around us, we children soon found new friends among the village children and found a paradise in and around the ruined fortress. We could explore the remnants of the old fortifications, the walls which must have surrounded the rooms, the courtyard, and the stables. What better place than here to reenact the magic of the knights and ladies of the Court—the obligatory evil sorcerer, the witches, and the hero who saves everybody in the end. Most of the ruins were overgrown with shrubs which soon yielded bucketfuls of raspberries, but also were the home of bees which once attacked us and we ran home covered with bee bites. Needless to say, there was no school in this final chaos of the war. We were not particularly sad about it. My mother, though, being a trained teacher, made sure that we did the homework which she left for us every morning before she took the milk down the mountain. She would give us some writing and arithmetic homework, and unless we had finished it by the time she came back, we were not allowed to go out to play. I kind of liked this form of homeschooling, being allowed to do it at my own speed; we also did a lot of drawing as long as we could get paper and colored pencils, but soon we ran out of paper too, and there were absolutely no books anywhere.

The three unmarried sisters, whom I mentioned before, were never able to get rid of their ugly, sour, grim faces—I never saw them smile. They worked very hard, though, making cheese, curd cheese, and butter from the cows' milk, spinning their own wool from sheep hair, and producing "Loden," an extremely durable form of wool cloth, by pressing sheep hair together with some simple chemicals and making jackets and men's pants from this material. I read later that this type of clothing went back thousands of years, and was perfectly adapted to the rough mountain climate, but was also worn in warmer regions of the Alpine countries. It is actually cool in the summers and warm in the winters and completely impermeable to water. Archeologists had found remnants of this clothing on Indo-European skeletons, thousands of years old in southern Russia, probably before Indo-European tribes spread out into India and into western Europe and the Mediterranean countries.

Suddenly one day at the end of May, rumor spread that Germany had capitulated and that Hitler and his companions had committed suicide. The Russian had occupied all of eastern Germany and Austria, and the western powers had moved eastward until they met the Red Army. Newspapers were not printed at that time, but some people had radios. All of a sudden, I saw truckloads of English soldiers arrive in our village. Nobody was afraid of the English, they did not bother anybody and were welcome by us. They set up camp in the village school and stayed pretty much out of sight of the population. Of course, I had to explore what they looked like and how they lived. I snuck into the school building and found young soldiers smiling at me. Unfortunately, I could not understand or talk with them. Hitler had discouraged the study of languages—interpreters were actually executed in some countries, when the Germans had to retreat. At one point, my mother had begun to teach us French, which I enjoyed enormously, but then, without an explanation, she stopped it. Today I know that she was probably warned, foreign languages were not allowed to be taught, because after the "Final Victory" German would be the only language to be used.

The British soldiers brought something else with them. They put up posters all over the villages with photos of the concentration camps, the skeleton-like humans, and the piles of emaciated dead corpses, and little children stretching out their spindly arms begging for food with features like old people. I had been secretly privy to the knowledge about the gas chambers after overhearing a conversation between my mother and my grandmother, but I had not been able to comprehend the horror of these concentration camps and the enormity of the crimes committed there. In later years, if anybody tried to tell me that the German people had never known about these crimes, I would tell them that I knew about the gas chambers at the age of seven. Another thing that I observed: On the Sunday immediately after the declaration of the fall of Germany, I saw many people whom I knew had been members of the Nazi party stand in front of the church in order to publicly demonstrate what good Christians they were, and that they had always attended Sunday services—something that Hitler had discouraged. Most people denied their membership in the Nazi party, destroyed their swastika badges, acted as if they had never known anything about the Nazi crimes and do so to this day. The fact is that every man who managed to stay at home instead of being sent to the front had been a member of the party, except for older farmers and doctors, and that everybody in a public function (police, school principals, University professors, storeowners, administrators, etc.) wore the swastika badge. There had also been people who had become very rich during the war by appropriating Jewish property or any property of so-called "enemies of the German Empire." It was at this time, when many war criminals tried to escape their deserved punishment by assuming false identities, or fleeing over the mountains into Italy where with the help of Pope Pius XII they ended up in Argentina, Chile, and Brazil. The British turned out to be good occupiers, except for one alcoholic among the troops whom I observed knocking on the doors of some houses asking for gin or whiskey, something that did not exist there at that time. I even made a friend among the British soldiers on my secret explorations of their camp. His name was Christian and he told me that he had a sister in England whose name was Elizabeth and that she was the same age as I. We exchanged some vocabulary, he taught me some English words and I taught him German words, and each time he gave me some chocolate and soap, both of which were huge treasures for us. My first words in English were "chocolate" and "Thank you." At that time, we could not even buy soap any more, which meant one could not wash clothes, dishes, or oneself. My aunts washed dirty dishes with sand, the clothes had to be boiled in water and then rinsed and wrung and hung outside for drying. It is amazing how little one really needs.

I do remember, however, that in the last years of the war, we bought a soap, called "Rifsoap," and rumor had it that it had been made from the bones of Jews in the concentration camps. It was hard as a rock, made without fat. Mutti did not allow us to use that soap. Shoes had also become more difficult to buy, so we too learned to take our shoes off on muddy streets and carry them until we reached an asphalt road where we could put them back on. All the stores were either closed or empty—a little later the Black Market began to flourish and one could buy anything for a wedding ring.

It soon became apparent that that the area where we lived was to become that part of Austria that the British would occupy, further west, around Salzburg, was to become the American sector, the westernmost part was to become the French sector. The entire eastern part of Austria would be occupied by the Russians, including the city of Vienna which would be divided among the four Victors like Berlin. I also learned that the name "Austria" would be returned after the Germans had called our country "Ostmark" (East land). This was now the third time that my citizenship changed. Born as Austrian, then forced to become a German citizen, then again Austrian. There were many rumors about the new government to be created. Some people hoped that the Habsburg family would come back from its exile in Switzerland and form a monarchy together with the surrounding countries along the Danube and into the Balkan. Naturally, the Sowjets would never have accepted that. Stalin really wished to integrate all of eastern Europe together with the eastern part of Germany and Austria into the Sowjet Union, and much more.

Once I saw the British soldiers destroy a wagonload full of furniture and household items, and a picture of Adolf Hitler. I am sure that these things must have belonged to a high Nazi who had tried to rescue his belongings by requisitioning an entire train wagon. The British burned the picture of Hitler and most of the furniture. The local people were busy grabbing clothes and household items. I somehow got hold of some children's clothes and shoes which I triumphantly carried home. We had grown out of most of our old clothes, and these things were more than welcome.

In the meantime, my sister and I had made many friends among the local children, many of whom were refugees too. I remember one boy from Latvia who was a kind of leader among us children. One day, he told me that his family would be sent back to Riga in Latvia, and that was the last I ever heard or saw of him. Later, I learned that many of these refugees had been collaborators of the Nazis and often ended up in Sowjet Prison camps.

We and most of our relatives were lucky to be generally healthy and in no need of medical treatments. At that time there were no antibiotics yet and I heard that some people died of infected blisters or pimples which turned into septicemia. Most of the medical doctors had either been sent to the front or were in prison camps, also there had been a high mortality rate of doctors during the fighting. Medical students, like my Uncle Hans, were trained early to take care of the wounded—later, when they were back at the Universities they must have passed their surgery examination with highest honors. When I began losing my primary teeth they were all pulled out with plyers which was no big deal for primary teeth, but I heard adults scream when they had to get their aching teeth pulled with plyers. Dental anesthesia was not introduced to Austria until the late 1950s and I could write volumes about having root canals performed without local anesthesia! Even major surgeries, like sinus operations, were performed without any form of anesthesia, but more about that later.

One or two days before the war officially ended, there was a major excitement. The family who had fled with us from the Russians, my Aunt Resi and her daughter Frieda with the baby, found out that Frieda's husband who had been a German soldier in Italy, had gone AWOL and was to be executed in a nearby village. He had probably tried to find his family. Frieda rode on her bicycle all the way to that village, and somehow, I have no idea how she did it, she got him out and home. In those days there was so much chaos—with gold and diamonds—money had become worthless—one could do anything.

Toward the end of the year, when it started getting colder in the mountains, my mother decided to take us back to Tautendorf and possibly even get us back into school. I don't remember how we travelled those two hundred miles—there were no cars, no trains, no buses, no more SS trucks. I remember vaguely that we spent some time on a wagon pulled by cows and we did a lot of walking. When we arrived in our old village, Tautendorf, all the houses were still there, nothing had been burned down. The farmers were beginning to repair their war damages and had even been able to harvest some fields. All our relatives were alive, but I overheard some grim tales about the Russian soldiers having raped all the women. I had no idea what "raping" meant, but assumed that it must have been something pretty awful while they forced the women's husbands, if they were alive, to watch. If somebody tried to defend their wives or if the dogs tried to protect them, they were simply shot. In our village they had shot all the cows, horses, and chickens for their own provisions. In the cities where people had water toilets, I was told, that most Russian soldiers had never seen such things, and thought that they were there for washing one's hair. They of course stole everything that they thought was of value to them. Their first demand was "ura," meaning they wanted one's wristwatch.

As far as children were concerned, I was told, that they never harmed any children, as opposed to the German criminal type of SS who had made it a sport to shoot Russian and Polish children while pretending to throw a ball and play with them.

At the years 1945 and 1946 the people in the cities suffered terribly of lack of food and supposedly, there were some people who starved to death. While still in the country, I saw people from the cities come into our villages to trade their wedding rings and other material belongings for a pound of lard and some apples. Many farmers became quite rich in those days and could soon fill their stables again with necessary farm animals. We lived again in our little room on Uncle Franz's farm where we had no food shortages except for luxury items, such as sugar. In the winter we went back to school in Soechau where I now was in fourth grade. Because all children had missed at least one year of school, they were all terribly behind academically, there were children in fourth grade who still could not read. Thanks to our Mutti's tutoring my sister and I were not behind, but we were bored in school. I had a young male teacher who had just returned from the war and a prison camp in the USA. He often told us what a wonderful country America is, read to us from his diary, and stressed, of course, how lucky he had been to end up in an American prison camp instead of a Russian one. I was so bored in school that my teacher announced to make me his assistant. He made me correct homework, write texts on the blackboard for others to copy, and read to the pupils. He also helped me prepare for my entrance examination into high school.

The first postwar year ended and it seemed to me that the whole area had recovered pretty well from the damage that the Russians had done. We too had lost all our clothes that we had left behind. I was very sad about one white silk dress that my mother had sewn herself. Later, my most favorite teacher in Vienna said to us that all mundane things can be lost so easily, whereas the only thing that cannot be stolen, is what is in one's brain, in other words, education. Considering the ravages of brain diseases, like Alzheimer's disease, even that is not so certain.

In those days, one had to take an entrance examination to get into high school. Later it was sufficient to have made good grades in grade school (elementary school) to be accepted into high school. High schools were and are meant to be an eight-year preparation for a University. The nearest place where they had a high school was in Furstenfeld, a town that had to be reached by train from Soechau, only a half-hour train ride. Needless to say, nobody owned a car. In my class in Soechau, there were only three of us who tried to take this examination. I am sure that there were many smart children in my class, but being almost exclusively farmers' children, they were not motivated to achieve anything academically. These exams were not easy and there was absolutely no material available to study from. I used one of my mother's handwritten notebooks with math problems, a book that she herself had used for her entrance exam. I worked hard on these problems, because, I think Math has never been my special talent, until I fell in love with calculus in our senior year of high school. Reading books was out of the question, because there were no books anywhere to be found. They had all disappeared from schools and libraries until many years after the war. First books had been examined by the Nazis if they fit into their ideology—everybody remembers the famous burning of books by the Nazis soon after Hitler had come to power. Then toward the end of the war, people had to use the paper from books for kindling of their primitive wood or coal stoves. Having prepared myself as well as I could, I did very well in my entrance exams. I liked both the pupils there and the teachers. I thoroughly enjoyed those two days in Furstenfeld and could barely wait to go to high school there. The teachers were mostly middle-aged men, or at least they appeared quite old to me as a ten-year-old. They were all very friendly and appeared to like me.

In the fall of 1946, my mother decided to move back to Vienna. We had found out that our apartment house in the 18th district was in the American sector and therefore it was safe to go back. Vienna, like Berlin, had been quartered by the four Victors. The eastern portion east of the Canal of the Danube, belonged to the Russian, the western areas belonged to the American, the British, and the French. It was not until the year 1956 when the occupation forces moved out and made a peace treaty with Austria in exchange for neutrality, similar to Switzerland. Germany, on the other hand, never got a peace treaty. Vienna had been seriously bombed; when we came back we saw many ruins where once there had been apartment buildings, and people were just beginning to rebuild. Even the 800-year-old St. Stephan's Cathedral had been burned out in the last days of the war. It took another ten years for this church to be repaired. One could easily walk through the western sectors, but in order to get into the Russian sector one needed a special ID card. Also people said that it still was not completely safe to walk there, because sometimes drunk Russian soldiers would harass people. The only time when we had to pass through the Russian sector, was when we visited my father's parents in Korneuburg at the Danube. I said already that the entire eastern part of Austria was occupied by the Russians, similar to East Germany. In the first years after the war, my grandparents had two Russian officers assigned into their house, into their spare bedroom, which was never heated. But my grandparents said that these two officers were highly educated and real gentlemen. Although the room where they stayed, was to my taste, really ugly and dark and cold, these two officers said that they had never lived in such a nice house before and regretted having to leave it when they were to go back to Russia. The American officers, on the other hand, lived in the most luxurious hotels in Vienna, drove their huge American cars, were well dressed and smelled of expensive tobacco.

Right after the war, both the Americans and the Sowjets created their own radio stations with the intent to influence the population politically. There were also suddenly many newspapers belonging to the various political parties: the Christian Democrats who held the majority of votes, the Socialists, and the Communists who had only a few votes in the Parliament. Immediately after the end of the war, the occupation forces helped Austria to establish its own government again. The first chancellor happened to be a survivor of a concentration camp who turned out to be an excellent negotiator with the Sowjets. The first president was a well-known Socialist, his name was Renner. The Communist newspapers and radio stations spoke enthusiastically about the "Workers' Paradise" in the Sowjet Union, and how it had been the Russians who had made every important invention scientifically, medically, technologically and humanistically. There were even special stores in the Russian sector where they sold food at very low prices, at a time when the population of the Sowjet Union was starving. All this was meant to be propaganda, of course, because Austria was meant to become part of the Sowjet Union, according to Stalin. The Catholic Church, I must admit, stood up against Communism, warned people from the pulpit not to shop in those "UNRA" (Russian) stores, not to believe Sowjet propaganda, and, hard to believe if I had not heard it myself, told women to get treatment for syphilis, which the Russian soldiers had spread. The Austrian Government introduced "Religion" as an obligatory subject in all schools. The Christian Democrats published an excellent newspaper, "Die Furche," propagated a form of humanistic capitalism with strong protection of the workers, got laws passed by Parliament to protect the poor, the sick, to give free education to all children all the way into the universities, and free medical care. If only the priests had been allowed to preach against Fascism from their pulpits ten years earlier!

Yet the Communists were very active with their propaganda. I remember some tenants in our apartment building knocking on all the doors with a so-called peace list to sign. These were exactly the same people who had been Nazis during the Hitler dictatorship. There was one family in which each family member belonged to a different party for protection: one was a Communist, one a Socialist, one a Christian Democrat. My family was certainly already on a "Black List" because my mother refused to sign the "peace list"—"peace" meaning nothing else but supporting the Communist party. By the way, by that time, we were beginning to get some tiny postcards from my father from his prison camp in Russia. At least we knew now that he was alive. We also received visits from unknown women who begged my mother to tell them anything about their lost husbands since we had received a sign of life from Papa, but he certainly would not have been allowed to talk about other men in those prison camps.

When we returned to our apartment in Vienna, at Anastasius Gruengasse 3, we found two elderly people living in the two middle rooms of our rather large apartment. They had been bombed out and of course, they needed a place to live. This was a common practice during the war. This meant for us that we had to use the outside corridor when we wanted to get from our kitchen and bathroom to our living and bedroom. This common corridor was cold in the winters, not too clean, and in general a big hassle. It was not until my father had returned from Russia in 1948, when these people moved out not without quite a bit of bureaucratic manipulating. Even though the apartment building where we lived belonged to my maternal grandparents, there was nothing that they could do. We thought that these people were Communists, and everybody was afraid of the Communists, who constantly said that they would take over eastern Austria and Germany.

Much later, in the year 1952, when I was an exchange student in Erie, Pennsylvania, I heard a lecture in my school by a man from the State Department in Washington, D.C. He talked about the "Cold War" and that the eastern part of Austria and Germany would soon go to the Sowjet Union. I remember that I felt terrible anguish. How Austria eventually achieved a peace treaty with the withdrawal of all occupation forces, is still a political miracle to me. The Russians did not have to go very far, they had their encampments right at the Hungarian border, some 40 miles east of Vienna. In case of a war within the long "Cold War" crisis, they could easily have been back in Vienna within two hours and at the Rhine river within one day. Austria had to commit itself to build up its own army, for defensive purposes only. We often joked about the three formidable tanks that this Army possesses.

In October 1946, after we had returned to our apartment in Vienna, which, by the way, had also been partially "relieved" of clothes, household articles, rugs, etc., I was allowed to choose between two high schools, both of which were at about the same distance from us. My grandmother had made inquiries and found out that the school in the 19th district catered to the upper-middle class, whereas the school in the 18th district was very strict academically. It was considered to be the strictest girls' school in Vienna. I chose the strict school. I had enough of the boredom and the doodling around from my elementary school in the country. This new school was indeed very challenging and I got out of the habit of always being the best "A" only student in school. But I was incredibly fortunate to get the best education from female teachers all of whom had made a doctorate in their specialties. Coming from an easy country school, I had to work hard indeed, particularly because I was one month late and had missed the beginning of the classes. There were moments when I thought that I could not make it, most of all, believe it or not, in English! But soon, I was making good grades again, and in my first report card, I brought home mostly "A's." Other girls, who were probably more intelligent than I, were either not attentive enough or did not care so much. I thoroughly enjoyed the high standard in every class, and later, in the upper classes, was actually glad, when some of the less interested girls left for the easier school in the 19th district. The teachers had to write everything on blackboards from which we had to copy, because there were still no books, no library, no gym until much later, no educational aids of any kind, no heating. We had to wear winter coats and gloves during the winter. Alas, nobody owned warm clothes and nothing could be bought in the empty stores. My mother did a lot of knitting, even our underwear was knitted out of a wool substitute. Most of the girls in our school had no fathers—I will talk more about that later—and they were all hungry.

For two years the Red Cross sponsored school lunch every day, where we got soup, cocoa, peas, and beans. Everybody complained in those days about hunger, and some girls were indeed quite malnourished. This was one reason why there was no physical education. Some of the girls were just too underweight to put any physical stress on their bodies. The school had a large gym hall with gym instruments, but due to the lack of heating, it was ice cold, which would have added additional stress on those frail bodies. I myself was lucky, I don't remember ever feeling hungry which might be a genetic trait of our family. Even my father wrote in his memoirs about his stay in Russian prison camps, that he felt less hunger than most of the other men there. In addition to that, nobody in our family was really tall—I was always the shortest kid in school—genes that perhaps go all the way back to surviving the great European wars and periods of starvation throughout history. I suffered much more from the poor or nonexistent heating during the cold seasons. Sometime during the years 1946-'47, public transportation was reinstalled in Vienna. It consisted of electric trains, the means of transportation before the war. They too were unheated and, of course, very crowded, because at that time almost nobody in Vienna owned a private car. We did not have to use public transportation, but could walk to school, in about 35-40 minutes, which was probably an excellent exercise and a mental preparation for school in the mornings.

I soon found out that even in our own classroom a bitter political battle was unfolding. These were the years 1948-1950 when we were in the second to fourth grade of high school.

Elizabeth Maria Schmid, M.D.

Most of the girls in my class came from families who had been high members of the Nazi party. I have already explained that these families had stolen the mansions of rich Jewish families who never returned from the concentration camps, and so these families could keep their stolen properties. Their fathers had been the intellectual elite within the Nazi party, or SS medical doctors, or even war criminals. Except for a few girls they all defended the Nazi ideology. Whenever our teachers touched the subject of the tragedy of the Jews, they became quite militant in terms of calling all this "Communist Propaganda" and that in reality no Jews were ever killed, or more cynically, that Hitler had not killed enough of them. Having seen with my own eyes those photographs of the concentration camps, as posted by the British in our village in May 1945, I began to defend what I was convinced was the reality of Auschwitz, Dachau, Bergen-Belsen, etc. It seemed to me that I was the only one who dared to fight this battle about the truth and some of the girls would fight pretty dirty. One incident: Our Latin teacher, who was a Catholic nun, always dressed in black with a big cross around her neck, mentioned the crimes against the Jews committed by the Nazis. She would more often speak about history and philosophy than about Latin Grammar—for which I am still grateful to her. My neighbor hissed to me in a low, but hateful voice: "Too bad he did not catch them all!" I got tears in my eyes which my teacher noticed. After class she called me to her desk and talked to me in an attempt to comfort me. From what I remember, she tried to explain to me that all these girls had been heavily indoctrinated by their parents and really did not understand what they were talking about.

Another thing on that subject, was that it was considered "cool" by those children to taunt our teachers sometimes to the point of cruelty, particularly our religion teacher. At that time I had not known that young Adolf Hitler was known to have been a very poor student academically and that he was a scourge for his teachers and particularly his religion teacher. He had made straight "F's" in all subjects in his school, until he dropped out after only six years of education. Even in the subject of "Behavior" for which we got a grade at that time he had received straight "F's," only in Physical Education he used to get "A's."

Our teacher in Religion was a Jesuit with two doctorates, one in Theology, one in Philosophy, and was also am accomplished cello player—needless to say, a highly educated intellectual. He was a big man with a broad back, onto which some girls would stick ridiculous cartoons when he had turned around or even shoot paper arrows at him, I was appalled by this behavior, but there was nothing I could have done. If I had told him, my own existence in that class would have become intolerable, because already, they secretly called me "The Communist." This situation became much better, after some of the worstgirls chose to leave our school and go to the school in the 19th district or somewhere else; they had been good students, so I have no idea why they chose to go to a different school.

Some of the girls in my class, even though they were the daughters of prominent Nazis, later turned out to be very nice human beings. One, however, whose father had been some kind of an SS man, became the female equivalent of a sociopath—a hysterical personality disorder with all kinds of psychosomatic complaints, early sexuality, even promiscuity and frequent vulgar speech. Another one manipulated and swindled her way through school by copying homework and tests from others, often from me, but she never achieved anything professionally later in life. There were two girls—I remember their names, Marschik and Hermsen—from Nazi families too, who introduced the novels of Karl May into our school. They even owned some of these books and we all wanted to be friends with them in order to borrow their books. Karl May's juvenile and silly novels used to be Adolf Hitler's favorite literature and he even read them as an old man, which reflects his immaturity and emotional retardation. Some of the girls became so addicted to reading these novels that they would secretly read them during class hidden underneath their writing papers. I myself began to like the fairytales about the Apache Chief Winnetou, but found the novels about the writer's supposed fantastic travels in Arabia and Kurdistan a bit silly and boring. Needless to say, in all these novels there was one good German hero who fought on the side of Winnetou against the American capitalists, Jewish fortune hunters, and other Indian tribes who were on the side of White Man. Karl May, by the way, spent most of his life in German jails for theft and wrote most of his adventure stories in jail with the help of maps of Arabia and the Southwest of the USA. These two girls also propagated a completely misunderstood Nietzschean philosophy, just like the Nazis had used

Nietzsche's words out of context, such as the "survival of the fittest," something that Nietzsche only referred to in the moral sense. As good Hitler girls they showed contempt of those girls who were athletically weaker. They could not do very much to me, because I was a good athlete and a good student, although what they liked to call a "Streber," a hardworking student. Nevertheless I was afraid of them and very happy when I found out that they would be leaving our school after the third grade. Things became more peaceful after that and the novels of Karl May became less and less interesting and soon fell into oblivion. Some girls used to read so-called girls' books which they had inherited from their grandmothers and which were unbearably sentimental. These girls too left our school after the fourth grade to go to a less academically challenging school. Both the third and the fourth grade we had to spend in a dark, cold room on the lowest floor of the building with hardly any view of the outside. There was hardly a day when I did not wish to be outside rather than inside. The all-over atmosphere in class became much better after the fourth grade, because only those girls remained who were intelligent and interested in learning something. This was fortunate because with the help of good teachers we developed a highly intellectual niveau with historical and philosophical discussion on a university level at the age of 16 years. Also, fortunately, there was absolutely no interest in boys, dating, dancing other than our formal dancing school. Fun were things like going to a theater performance, to classical concerts, a good film, and even to evening classes in the local community college for adults. At one lecture about the Sistine Chapel in the Vatican, the lecturer referred to us as "children" who should not be present in an adult class—typical, surly behavior frequently found in Vienna. Many tourists think that Viennese people are friendly, but foreigners who live there long enough, find out that the typical Viennese is not friendly at all, Xenophobic, contemptuous of anything different, haughty, class conscious, arrogant toward lower classes who themselves are money hungry, and terribly vulgar when under the influence of alcohol which one sees frequently.

Slowly we had more access to books, stores were stocked again, food became plentiful, and our classrooms were well heated, still by primitive coal stoves which had to be taken care of by a special attendant. At least one could bake apples on these stoves which filled the rooms with delicate odor. Latin became one of my favorite subjects, because I enjoyed the logical structure of Latin grammar and sentences. With Math I had to struggle a bit, had to invest more energy and time in order to get good grades. Once in fourth grade I nearly flunked a written math test, out of five grades, I made a four which made me deeply ashamed. At home, my father had already come back from the Russian prison camps, he sat down with me and taught me the fundamentals of logical thinking in Math, such as writing equations correctly and slowly, and going meticulously from line to line in order to achieve the correct result. I will always be grateful to my father for teaching me slow, methodical, step-by-step thinking. May he have found the best place in Heaven! I employed this method of thinking in every other subject afterwards, and it made studying much easier and much more fun. Soon I came home with an "A" on my next written Math test.

As I had already mentioned we were extremely lucky with our teachers in school, one in particular. She was our teacher in Geography and History. Not only were her classes on a university level. She lectured to us and we would take notes. I think she did not believe much in schoolbooks, which we did not have anyway. So I learned at the age of 11 and 12 already to take notes from lectures and because of this I hardly ever had to study from these notes at home, because once you write things down you remember them so much better. Her lecturing style was like storytelling, it made us all sit on the edges of our chairs with attention and waiting for the ending of the beautiful story. I will never forget how she made us appreciate something as dull as Lower Austria without slides, photos, just one worn-out school map. She described the mountains and valleys so vividly that I could have painted them. Needless to say she was also a great traveler and hiker and had seen so much of Austria herself that she could paint the landscapes with her speech. History was even more exciting. I will never forget her stories about the war between Rome and Carthage. In addition, it seems that our teachers, because it was a small school, could coordinate their schedules. When we learned in History about something, our Latin teacher would talk about the same subject. So in some respects our school was a model for the Walddorf schools where pupils get fully involved in a certain time period from all possible perspectives. She would also read to us from famous historical books. Scipio, Hannibal, the Emperor Fredric II, Charlemagne, Socrates, became my personal friends. But even there I later realized that she slanted things according to her own Germanic concept—I suspect she must have been in the Hitler Youth ten years earlier. The "blue eyes" of Scipio—the Roman general—overwhelming the "brown eyes" of the Semitic Hannibal. Or the 12-cent German Hohenstaufen Emperor Fredric II who grew up in Sicily, because that was the personal fiefdom of his family, being a leader of the black-haired children in Sicily. Our Biology teacher, who was a Catholic nun, told us how Negroes were racially inferior to white people and having a different body odor. They did not know any better, this was the way they had learned things themselves. An unforgettable experience was a summer camp in Rimini near Ravenna, Italy, with this beloved teacher, when I was about 14 years old. We stayed in a sort of hostel right next to the ocean surrounded by Italian children, Italian cuisine, Italian teachers. It was there where I learned my first Italian. When other girls slept or chatted I would study Italian vocabulary. I think during all these years of high school my classmates tolerated me with a slight respect for my fervor in studying and an admirable acceptance of my mild eccentricities, partially because I was totally harmless and partially because I helped anybody who asked me for a favor. I was also always the smallest kid in class, the tiniest eater, the least developed physically, the plainest dressed, quiet, and well behaved. Today they would call me a "nerd." Once in Italy, Dr. Krainer, that was her name, took me and three others on a special trip to Assisi. For days she prepared us in detail about the history, St. Francis, the architecture that we were about to see, and it was still overwhelming for me to actually be there and see all this beauty. The second unforgettable sight was Venice on the way back to Vienna. I thought I was in Heaven, I had not imaged how stunningly beautiful the cathedrals and historic buildings were.

While the other girls bought little trinkets, scaffoletti (little scarfs), with their spending money I bought color postcards with the intention of sharing them with my parents after my return and telling them about all these wonderful things that I had seen.

Right after the war, we went several times to summer camps organized by the Jesuits of our Church, which hardly cost anything.

They were actually meant to feed the starving children, but since we never starved we did not need these camps for food but they turned out to be great adventures. We would hike for hours every day as a group usually singing and carrying the flag of our church. Then we made campfires and would tell stories. There was one priest who would tell us the most horrific medieval folktales, of heroes and appearance of the devil and angels, of ladies in the fortresses being strangled by ghosts. Once we were invited by a monastery where a nun had just died. We were allowed to see her lying in her coffin. These experiences cannot even be reconstructed in film any more. We truly lived in a medieval culture with all the smells, the superstitions, the total absence of machines, cars, electricity.

The day my father came home from Russia must have been late in 1948. There had been transports of prisoners of war since 1946, but we did not get any information about Papa until probably 1947 or so. Sometimes strangers rang our doorbell asking if our father had come back and if my mother knew anything about their relatives. People were so desperate to get any news from Russia. When we got the first postcard from Russia and knew that he was alive we expected Papa to return soon. But it still took quite a while. Stalin made the prisoners of war build entire Russian cities and the rail tracks and did not let them go home until Russia was somewhat repaired. I felt the excitement when the day approached when Papa would be one of the returned men. We were in the living room and I had prepared a little song on the piano that according to Mutti he had always liked. He walked in with her and I saw a man that I had never seen before. He was in a shabby, dirty Russian soldier-like uniform in grey. I think Mutti later took that uniform away from him and I never saw it again. He carried a duffle bag filled with old, stale bread. His idea was to bring us something to eat because in Russia they had been told how hungry we were at home. He had actually saved his rations of bread for several days in order to bring us something to eat. Each time I think of this I still cry. I knew instantly that this man was a thoroughly good person and in a way a hero. But I also felt instantly that this man had no clue what to say to us, how to approach us—we were strangers. More, there was suddenly somebody who claimed to own Mutti—when in reality we owned her—and who said that he was our father. I remember that he tried to tell us a little about where he had been, but I don't remember much more. I think he was so hungry and tired that he needed to rest and eat for several days.

My and my sister's life became more difficult with Papa at home.

My mother had been very clever and assertive to get herself and us through the war without Papa around. Now, it seemed to me that he tried to recapture his position as "pater domini" (the ruler of the house) in the style of the 19th century. He made us ask for permission to do the most harmless things, like attending a stage theater, and sometimes he would actually say NO. Once I wanted to join a gym class outside of school, in the evenings. He claimed that all these gym schools were run by Socialists (before the war, most had actually been organized by the Socialists) and would under no conditions allow us to join some "red" organization. Finally he agreed to go with us to that gym school to talk to the director there. He found out that this school had no political connections whatsoever, and so we were allowed to join. Papa had a visible hatred for the Austrian Socialists which I could not understand because in Russia he had been permitted to attend a Communist School which had not only saved his life, but also gave him a solid foundation in the principles of Marxism. I found out that he principally agreed with Karl Marx, but from the Catholic point of view.

As food became more plentiful, we developed a big issue at the dinner table. Mutti had a live-in maid by that time and together they cooked very good meals. We had "family dinner" each evening in our living room. Papa must have felt in Heaven to eat enough and well-cooked dinners, and he wanted us to feel the same way. Mutti slowly gained so much weight that she did not fit into her old clothes any more, and complained about her weight all the time. My sister Elfi too gained weight and developed quite womanly at the age of 12 or 13 years. Food had never had any particular fascination for me, and also I did not want to become fat so I began refusing to eat what was served on my plate. So the discomfort of our daily family dinners began. Papa tried to force me to eat, sometimes even slapping me, but I said NO. I tried to bribe Mutti into serving me only tiny portions, but even these were too much for me. This went on for about three years; today my refusal to eat would be called "Anorexia Nervosa"; it clearly was my way of opposing what I considered my father's unjust assumption of dominance over our family and interfering with everything I did. I even "forgot" to eat my breakfast at home or to bring my lunch to school, and would not eat anything all day long in order to be able to eat at least something at our awful dinners. As a result I became thin and did not grow much. If they had treated me with benign neglect I would probably have eaten quite normally and would have become bigger and taller. Soon Papa began harassing my sister for being fat, wearing her hair long, wearing more womanly clothes—what else could she have worn? There were no teenage fashions in Austria at that time. I asked her only some years ago how much she remembered of those dinners, but she seemed to have forgotten everything. My interpretation is that she had repressed those memories deeply in her unconscious, in order to retain a favorable image of our Papa. In terms of school, he could not harass me because I continued to bring home good grades, sometimes even the best report card of my entire class. In terms of clothes he could not harass me because I owned only two dresses, one green, one blue one, and showed absolutely no interest in clothes. In terms of "womanly" appearance he could not harass me because I was thin and tiny and wore glasses, looking more like a "nerdy" child.

Another war that my Papa had to fight was a political one. When he returned from Russia, lo and behold, most of the higher positions in the government, industry, and at the universities had already been given to others, even to former Nazis. He had to go back to his old job at the university pharmacy without doing research, not what he had expected as a "Nazi Victim." He became angrier and angrier when he noticed how these former Nazis had spent the entire war at the "homefront," in a warm, clean bed, with enough food, a good job, and no punishment after the war. Whereas he and many others who had returned late from Russian prison camps could not find the kind of jobs which they would have enjoyed, if they had not wasted seven or more years in Russia. I remember him as a very angry man with possibly a mild form of posttraumatic stress disorder, which was, of course, not recognized then.

Even though I was thin and tiny, I was a good athlete in school and could hike for hours. Once while on a vacation with an aunt in Salzburg, I persuaded Papa and my sister to hike to a famous ice cave in the mountains near Salzburg. This was a hike of several hours carrying on our backs heavy backbags filled with warm clothes for the ice caves. Papa soon became dizzy and almost fainted and my sister played lazy. So I had to carry three heavy backbags, one on my back, one in the front, and one in my hands, and we made it to the caves. I recognized then that my Papa was in poor physical condition probably as a result of his life in Russia. I also recognized that I, as thin as I was, was in excellent athletic condition. In school, we played a lot of silly ballgames, which I hated, because I could rarely catch the ball with my nearsighted eyes, but when it came to instruments, like the parallel bars, the rings, the ladders and ropes, I was like a little fly, far ahead of the others. We got one week of ski instructions each winter in a village in the mountains, where we lived in a hostel and had daily lessons in skiing by our gym teachers. I had to use old skis from my uncle and had ski boots in which I froze my toes. Our gym teachers were not good skiers themselves, so nobody learned how to ski, but we enjoyed the beautiful mountains and getting to know each other and the teachers better. My grandfather, who was a trained shoemaker, made me my first pair of ski boots—a pure act of love by him. He had, however, no idea what a good ski boot ought to look like, and made them much too narrow and low, which made it impossible to wear warm socks inside.

When I was about 14 or 15 years old, I overheard some girls say that they wanted to transfer to an art school which provided a normal high school graduation, but in addition to that training in graphical art and painting. I had always been interested in art, and made excellent grades in art class. But that does not mean much. Our art teacher was an artist herself, but restricted us to photorealistic drawing and painting. I had no idea that anything else existed. The museums in Vienna showed exclusively classical and baroque art. I did not know any art galleries which would have shown more modern art and did not even know that there had been a lot going on in the artworld since the turn of the century. Hitler had forbidden any modern art and so our museums were depleted of modern art even five years after the end of the war. I do remember that I felt transformed whenever I stood in front of a painting by Rafael or da Vinci, like stepping into a fantastic world. I loved the theater which played mostly classical plays or plays from the 19th century. This feeling of a sudden transformance happened to me when I saw for the first time the play "Waiting for Godot" by Beckett. I recognized that there were things out there which I had never known in my limited world.

Not only had Adolf Hitler driven away or executed the best German scientists, he had also got rid of all modern art and artists, with few exceptions as long as they became members of his party, like the music conductors Herbert von Karajan and Furtwangler. It took an entire generation after the war to catch up with the rest of the world in terms of creating more modern art, music, poetry, prose. To think that the German-speaking countries had been intellectual and artistic leaders before Hitler had come to power!

When I mentioned at home that I was interested in an artistic career, I could just as well have said that I was going to fly to the moon. Papa even refused to talk about it, because he had decided that I would become a university professor in Medicine, Law, or Chemistry, or at least have a successful practice in Medicine. Can I say that my artistic career was stunted from the beginning? What did I know about my real talents or interests? At the age of 15 years one does not know oneself. Also I did not really want to leave my beloved school, except for that dark, cold classroom. My Mutti had always said that girls must learn a profession and be economically self-sufficient, and never, ever have to rely on a man for support. The way she used to say this, it sounded as if marriage for economic reasons was the most disgusting, humiliating, deplorable, stupid thing a woman could ever do. So much for an artistic career in which one would probably not earn enough money, and be either poor for the rest of one's life or having to marry a disgusting man. I think she always had little appreciation for men in general, and really was convinced that a woman can do a better job at almost anything and that men are completely redundant and unnecessary, a nuisance at best. Needless to say, I stayed in my school and gave up any idea of ever doing anything else but Medicine or Law or perhaps becoming a high school teacher.

Becoming an Exchange Student in America

This is how it happened. In 1951 I heard a rumor that the sister of one of my classmates had been selected to spend one year in the USA, so I became aware that there existed some programs which sent European students to the USA for studying, but soon forgot all about it.

Suddenly in the spring of 1952—we were just in music class listening to the 5th Symphony by Beethoven—the so-called "Destiny Symphony" whose first chords said "Victory" in Morse code—when somebody from the principal's office knocked at the door and called me to the principal. I was not aware of any misdemeanors, so I walked there with great curiosity. Our principal was a charming, young woman, our former gym teacher. She informed me that the Teachers' Conference had decided that I had been selected for an exchange student scholarship to the USA which would begin in the fall of 1952. I ran home with great excitement—we did not have a telephone then and very few people did. I needed my mother to come with me to school to give her signature and permission to let me apply. She came with me and very proudly signed all the necessary paperwork. I know that my teachers had not selected me because I was the most intelligent girl in class, but I was obedient, hardworking, curious, and had always shown empathy for those teachers who had been harassed by some of the Nazi girls. Politically, I was a good bet too. My father had a document which said that he had been a victim of the Nazis, which had given him some advantages in terms of taxes, school money, and even with theater tickets, if he had ever bothered to go to a theater. My teachers knew that I would behave well in America and not be a shame to Austria, and that I could adjust well in different circumstances and that my English was fairly good. There was a second girl who was eventually selected by a religiously sponsored exchange program, whereas mine was privately funded and government approved, the so-called American Field Service (AFS). I later learned that AFS selected only few and only the most highly recommended students into their program. I would be interviewed sometime by the American Embassy. My English teacher gave me a book to read about the USA (I think it was by Stephen Vincent Benet) and encouraged me to quickly read other books in English and also Austrian newspapers. The interview at the American Embassy could have been a bit frightening, but it turned out to be a lot of fun. I had just recently got my long braids cut and got a permanent—how stupid! The moment I entered the room with the big round table with many U.S. officials sitting there, they all burst out into a giggle because I looked so different from the photo that I had sent them before. I remember that I could understand their English quite well, although in school we had learned the British accent. Then they asked me all kinds of questions about which books I had read in English and about Austria in general, and a bit about politics. Thanks to my English teacher's advice I could give them a long list of books that I had read from the America House, and they did a bit of giggling again. One of them asked me, if by any chance I knew what the "Schuman Pact" was. By pure coincidence, our history teacher had mentioned that pact as a precursor to a possible European Union, beginning as a treaty between Germany and France, concerning the partition of coal in the Ruhr Area at the river Rhine. I could see in their faces that they were impressed. One of them actually stood up and congratulated me by saying that I was the first student who could answer that question. They promised that I would certainly be one of the students going to America in fall. I spent the next summer vacation reading English books exclusively and even attended some classes at the "America House" to practice my English and to learn more about America. By the end of the summer I received a letter telling me that I would be living with Mr. and Mrs. Skala in Lawrence Park, a suburb of Erie, Pennsylvania, and that I would be leaving at a certain date in August.

One requirement for obtaining a visitor's visa to the USA was getting a small pox vaccination. My mother took me to our family doctor for this, even though I had received a small pox vaccination as a young child. When this doctor found out that I needed the vaccination for a visa to the USA, he suddenly became red in his face with anger and screamed to my mother how could she be so stupid to let me go to America, which is a completely "Jewish" country, where all those Jews whom Hitler unfortunately had not destroyed were now living and controlling the world economy, just like they had done before.

We were both speechless and literally fled from this doctor's office. We soon found another doctor who was very willing to give me the small pox vaccination and even wished me good luck on my upcoming adventure.

In August, we were told to meet at the City Hall for further instructions. There was a large group of girls and boys of my age. I found out that only seven had been selected by AFS, the others were sponsored by different church groups and the Kiwanis club. I liked all the people in that group and made some friends who remained friends for many years to come. My parents did not have to pay anything, everything had been paid for by the sponsoring organizations. My mother quickly sewed me some new clothes, because I still had only two dresses, the green and the blue one. She could have saved herself the effort, because clothes were quite different in America where they had actually special clothes for teenagers. But neither my mother nor I knew that and she wanted me to make a good impression in America.

Our AFS group left Austria at the end of August. We took the train first to Cherbourg, France, then the "Queen Mary" from Cherbourg to New York. During the train ride already I felt unusually comfortable with the other six AFS candidates. They were all so intelligent and very nice. One of the girls was the Austrian ice skating champion, another one was the daughter of a famous actors' couple in Vienna, the equivalent of Lawrence Olivier in England. Elizabeth Hoerbiger herself became an actress many years later in Austria. There was a short guy with a pronounced accent from a certain industrial area of Vienna, Ottakring, apparently not from an elegant family, but I took an immediate liking to him and we remained good friends for the rest of his short life. He too happened to become a psychiatrist later and was well known as an excellent and compassionate doctor. Much later, he helped me emotionally in difficult stages of my own life. His name was Guenther Pernhaupt. One boy was there from Furstenfeld, the town where I had taken my entrance examination into high school some six years ago. One came from the most western region in Austria, from Vorarlberg, another one from the easternmost area near the Hungarian border, one from the mountains in Steiermark, where we had outwaited the war. I could tell that there were really the "cream of the crop," all were funny, witty, considerate to each other. It was pure joy to be with such a fine group of young people. The voyage on the "Queen Mary" took five days and that was considered the fastest way to cross the Atlantic. We were of course assigned to the lowest floor on the boat, near the engine rooms. There were two to each cabin which was without a porthole. I became seasick immediately. I don't remember ever having been so sick in my life; there were moments when I wished myself dead. During the entire trip I could barely eat anything, even though the food in the dining room and in the buffets looked delicious and quite foreign. Being third-class passengers, we were not supposed to go upstairs into the upper classes of the boat, but, needless to say, we snuck in. I was overwhelmed by the luxury of the dining rooms, the dance halls.

The elegantly dressed passengers spoke mostly French or English. The weather, I remember was stormy and cold, which is probably the reason why I became so seasick. When I could finally eat something, it was mostly ice cream, a luxury to me, and on top of that I could eat as much as I wanted to. When we approached New York, we saw the Statue of Liberty literally appearing out of the fog. I will never forget that sight. The arrival in the harbor of New York was tumultuous, loud, and chaotic. Fortunately, we were quickly rounded up by some volunteers from AFS, given something to eat, and taken by bus to the headquarters of AFS in downtown Manhattan. This was a small, old house, which has in the meantime been replaced by a skyscraper. The directors of AFS, Mr. Galati and Mrs. Field, welcomed us with great sincerity and took a personal interest in each of us. Mrs. Field took one look at my clothes and then invited me to a room with donated dresses, from which I could select as many as I wanted to, which I did. I loved these American teenage dresses, which were made for my age group, not for old women, I loved the long skirts which were fashionable in 1952, the blouses with short or no sleeves, the cute shoes. I put my

Austrian clothes away, the skirts which my mother had sewn, because they were short and well, too European. We were shown around New York for a few days, while we stayed in an old hotel whose name was "Martha Washington." At that time, New York was not dangerous yet. Nobody warned us of crime, muggings, kidnappings. With commonsense precautions one could walk just about everywhere. A group of us took off to visit the Statue of Liberty by ourselves and asked people for directions which they gave us with a friendly smile. However, in the end we missed the boat which should have taken us to the small island with the Statue. After some very happy days, one by one departed for their destinations. I found out late that I had been assigned together with an Austrian boy to the same family. The reason that was given was that Mr. and Mrs. Skala originally had wanted only one girl, but they could not find another family for the boy and so they decided to take both of us. His name was Herbert Hausmaninger. Of all the people in our group, he was the one whom I liked least of all. He was very tall, whereas I was very short; he had a big chin and little charm. We looked kind of funny together, he so tall and me so little. He was also very smart and certainly let me know it! Later he became a professor of Roman Law at the University of Vienna.

Mr. and Mrs. Dan Skala
1953

I often wished that I had landed with a family who had a girl of my age. I had no other choice but get along with him. Mr. and Mrs. Skala were both high school teachers and very idealistic Americans. They were both second-generation Americans from Scottish and Czech origins. They had been taking foreign students into their home for two years and planned on doing so in the future. They themselves were childless. They lived in a beautiful home directly on the shore of Lake Erie. Their home was equipped with all the modern miracles, like a washing machine, a dishwasher, a telephone, central heating, a car in the garage, a refrigerator with a freezing compartment. I got my own room for the first time in my life. If I had been sent to another planet, it could hardly have been much different for me. After all, it was only seven years after the war, Vienna was still partially in ruins, the stores had very limited selections of everything, although we were no longer hungry, economically more like a country from the Third World. When Aunt Jessie, that is what I called Mrs. Skala, took me for the first time to a department store, I could not believe my eyes when I saw the mass of goods that were sold even in minor stores, like Woolworth's. If I had had any money, I would have bought a lot of unnecessary and worthless things just for the sake of buying something for the first time in my life. By the way, AFS gave us a monthly allowance of pocket money, something like $15 per month. That is probably the equivalent of $150 today, enough to buy some clothes, underwear, some toilet articles, and small gifts. The food stores were filled to the brim with delicious things that I had never seen or heard of. Today I know that in those days Americans ate a very unhealthy diet, such as pure white bread, margarine (it was advertised as being healthier than butter), canned goods, factory-made foods, a lot of fat milk (skim milk was not sold then), and ketchup on everything. Aunt Jessie cooked dinner every day after work, but it usually came out of a box or can, the dishes were washed after dinner in a dishwasher, and so she managed without a maid and could work as English teacher at our high school. Toward the end of the year she became ill with pneumonia. So Uncle Dan, as we called Mr. Skala, did the cooking and the washing and everything. He was the principal of our high school and really a very nice man. It was here and then, when I saw a man do all the housework for the first time in my life. My father at home probably could not even boil an egg for himself. At that time we still had a live-in maid in Vienna. Before I knew that in America everything is washed in a machine, I once soaked my clothes in the bathtub overnight, because this is what we did in Vienna. Then the next day the washing woman would come to work all day and hang the washed clothes on lines in the attic. Mr. and Mrs. Skala got a big laugh out of this and often giggled later on when they told their family and friends about this. To them, I might as well have come out of the African Bush.

Otherwise, I soon got to appreciate modern technology. The central heating in the house and in school was wonderful, I never felt cold, even though at that time the girls used to wear white bobbysocks on naked legs instead of stockings or pantyhose. But the long coats protected us from the cold and then we were in warm schoolrooms or in warm houses. I don't remember that I ever froze during that year, although the climate in northern Pennsylvania is almost Canadian, that is cold. In school the classrooms were bright, clean with modern tables and chairs. There was a library with hundreds of books and I felt like a kid in a candy store, not knowing which books to select. In class we got schoolbooks which we were to take home each day. In the beginning I did not quite know what to do with schoolbooks and waited for the teachers to tell us the stories, until I noticed that the teachers expected us to read certain paragraphs in our books and be prepared the next day for a discussion or for a quiz. The name of this high school was Lawrence Park High and had, of course, a football team, a basketball team, a track team for the boys only. The girls were not allowed to play any sports, not even to run and the "gym classes" were a euphemism for playing a bit with a ball and taking a shower. There were no real gym instruments in the huge gymnasium with a shining wood floor. That was the only disappointment so far. Most of the people who lived in Lawrence Park were employed by General Electric which had a huge plant there. During my entire year there, I never saw an Afro-American or Hispanic American, or Chinese or Japanese or Native American. There was a main street with little shops and a famous milk bar, where we students used to assemble after school in order to drink milkshakes, play the jukebox and dance the jitterbug. I could not get used to American popular music or to dances which I had never seen before. I had heard only classical music in Vienna, some folk music, some church music, and the occasional Vienna operetta. The social life of the American teenager remained a riddle to me. I had never before heard of "dating," something that seemed to be the main interest of American teenagers. Also I found it difficult to put up with the teenage boys who seemed to have very limited interests, such as sports, dates with girls, and I am sure, how to buy alcohol, secretly. Pennsylvania was a "dry" state at that time. One could not officially buy alcohol. Most people and particularly young boys had to drive something like 50 miles to the border of New York State. When they drove home drunk, they sometimes had terrible accidents.

One of the first things that Mr. and Mrs. Skala showed us was a car wreck in which several teenagers from our school had died while driving drunk. Alcohol was the secret vice that many boys indulged in, perhaps because it was forbidden in the state of Pennsylvania. As far as I know these were no other illegal substances used in our area in the year 1952. Mr. and Mrs. Skala told us each day at dinner what a wonderful country America was, and for them it was indeed being only second-generation Americans. We also often talked about the "Cold War" and I assume that Mr. and Mrs. Skala really did not know about the crimes which were being committed at that time on both sides. Compared to the average American they were both very well educated, loved to attend concerts of classical music, and taught us surprisingly much about English and American literature—that was because Mrs. Skala was also our English teacher. They also took us to the high school football games and made us watch the big national baseball events. To this day, I have no idea what I had been watching, and still don't understand these games. The immersion in Lawrence Park High School was both traumatic and exciting. In the beginning I had problems with the American language as spoken by the average person. I am sure that I missed a good part of what was said in the classes and among the students in school. For instance, in our History class, which had been so exciting in my school in Vienna, I could not understand my teacher almost during the entire year, and other than what I read in my history book, I learned nothing in that class. The same thing happened in a class called "Problems of Democracy." They could just as well have spoken Chinese there! The concept of the American type of democracy was so foreign to me that in addition to language difficulties, I could not understand the concept. I took mostly classes that I could not have got in Europe, such as typing, and am glad to this day that I learned how to type with the ten-finger system. That helped me later many times, when I had to work as a secretary. We had a class called "Home Economics," where we learned the basics of housekeeping (the American way, of course) and cooking which I hated. Physical education was a joke. Girls in the 1950s in the USA were supposed to become housewives and mothers, maybe work in an office until they got married, or perhaps go to a college in order to find a husband there. Girls were not supposed to be athletic. I even suspected that the girls made fun of my well-developed muscles. Twice Uncle Dan (Mr. Skala) took me to a college in Pennsylvania where I was allowed to stay for a few days and attend college classes. They were much more interesting than the high school classes and the teachers were all very friendly and helpful. The college grounds and dormitories were well kept and luxurious in my eyes; there was even a buffet where one could eat whatever one wanted. However, the girls did not seem to be interested in learning anything. All they talked about, was boys, dates, school dances, clothes, all things that I was minimally interested in. Soon, back in Vienna, I found out that the number of Medical students at the University of Vienna was equal to the number of male students, and that in the Sowjet Union most of the doctors were female. There was only one girl in my Lawrence Park High School who was intellectual and very smart. She told me things about America that nobody else talked about, such as the lynchings in the southern states, the "apartheid" between black and white Americans, the fact that black Americans were not allowed to attend "white" schools, the enormous difference between the very rich and the poor who lacked health insurance, the CIA crimes all over the world and much more. She later joined the "Hippie" movement and the protests against the Vietnam War and for Civil Rights. Another girl in my class, Janet, was probably the most intelligent girl in school. She had a boyfriend, Bob, who was also smart, but maybe a little less than she, and in order to keep him as a boyfriend and to marry him after graduation, she played "dumb," and voluntarily made poorer grades on her tests than Bob in order not to intimidate him. After graduation, instead of becoming a

73

doctor or engineer, or going into the Foreign Service, she just attended a Homemaking Academy for girls. I hope that she never regretted it.

In the year 1952 I witnessed the election campaign between Eisenhauer and Stevenson. One day, I saw President Truman come into Erie on a train to give a speech in favor of Adlai Stevenson. He was accompanied by his daughter, who was a famously bad singer, and both looked to me completely unimpressive. To think that he had been the man who had released the atom bombs over Japan and won the War in the Pacific! At that time the USA was involved in the Korean War, and Eisenhauer, whom I also happened to see personally when he came through Erie, promised to "bring the boys home from Korea" and the rest is history. I know that Mr. and Mrs. Skala were Republicans and so was everybody else in Lawrence Park, it seemed to me. They often told us about the benefits of working for "Big Industry" like General Electric or the auto companies who paid good salaries, and even gave their employees medical insurance and pension plans, something that was taken for granted in all European countries. They even mentioned those factories where workers could live in factory owned housing and had very good lives there. Today I have heard these companies referred to as "slave plantations." Almost all people I talked with were really convinced that America was by far the best country in the world and it would be of great benefit to humanity if all the countries in the world would do as America did.

One of the best experiences during my year in Erie were frequent invitations to give talks about our exchange program and about Austria in general. I talked in many schools throughout Pennsylvania, to all kinds of clubs and cultural organizations. I was often asked about my experiences during the war, what I knew about the Jews, and about my father in Russian prison camps. I came to like talking publicly and this has stayed with me to this day. The idea of international student exchange was primarily an idealistic one. Bringing students to the USA, most likely students who would become future leaders in their own countries someday, and sending American students to overseas countries would serve toward better understanding between all the people of this world. Indeed, many of these exchange students later became leaders in their own countries. I know of several who became important in Germany, others became diplomats, or leaders in science and in the humanities. One girl from my school in Vienna later became a well-known politician in Austria. We were considered to be "little ambassadors" from our respective countries. One of the nicest visits was one to Pittsburgh, PA, where I stayed with a family and attended Monroe High School and gave many talks to the students, another one in good memory was to a high school in Harrisburg, PA. I noticed that many questions about life in Europe was about "dating." American students were truly surprised to hear that dating in the American sense did not exist in European countries. Girls were not supposed to go out alone with a boy, unless the parents were present.

One of the nicest people I met during my year in America, was Miss Keep, a Social Worker. I called her "Aunt Kathryn." She was unmarried, middle aged, lived with her mother. Her father was supposed to have been a big shot in the FBI in Washington, D.C. She truly loved young people and invited Herbert and me frequently out to dinners, cultural events, or to her home. We remained friends for the rest of her life. She told me that she could never remain involved in a relationship with a man because her father had to move so often and would take his family with him each time. She eventually adopted a baby girl and became a grandmother and great-great-grandmother to dozens of children.

Another interesting family that I met in Erie, was a Jewish family from Hungary. Once I was interviewed by a newspaper reporter about the exchange program and this article was published in a local paper. Soon I was contacted by this Jewish family who had a girl of my age, named Daisy. She was very beautiful. She and her family had survived the war in Budapest by changing their identity to a Christian one. Her mother was blonde and blue-eyed and got away as Non-Jewish, whereas her father had been taken to a concentration camp and had never come back. This was the first time in my life that I had personal contact with Jewish people who invited me to their holidays and their son's Bar Mitzvah. At that time I was still a devout Catholic and had to get permission from the local parish priest to attend Jewish ceremonies. Daisy told me a lot about being Jewish during the war. We remained in contact for many years, but then I lost her because both she and I changed our addresses quite frequently.

In my high school in Lawrence Park, I attended both junior and senior classes and graduated at the end of the schoolyear, typically in those white gowns, a silly hat, and high heels. The high school prom was a bit of a problem for me, because I did not have a date, nor had I ever had one before. So Herbert helped me out by asking one of our seniors, a nice, but somewhat dull boy, to be my prom date. Miss Keep bought me a formal dress, a beautiful, golden colored dress with lace. Back in Vienna, this dress became quite a sensation when I wore it to those elegant dances in the Emperial Palace during the Carneval season. Once a photographer even took photos of it. Everybody liked it, but it did look different from what was worn in Vienna at that time—well, very American!

At the end of the schoolyear, in June 1953, all AFS students were invited to the headquarters in New York, from where we began a one-month-long trip by Greyhound bus through a number of eastern and southern states. We stayed with American families who hosted us in different towns. This trip was a unforgettable experience. Wherever we spent time with families, we talked about the future of Europe and America until late into the nights, until we all ended up with sleep deprivation. We visited Lincoln's birthplace in Illinois (Chicago), then south to West Virginia, where I stayed with a Ku Klux Klan family. The man of the house proudly showed me his white robe and hat. When I asked him why he hated Negroes so much, he said that they were "lazy." That was exactly what a boy had told me in 1945, when I watched him play with a wooden gun pointed at imaginary Russians. I asked him why he wanted to shoot Russians, he said that they deserved to die because they are "lazy."

In Washington, D.C., a small group of us was taken to the Senate and presented to the then youngest Senator, John F. Kennedy. There was some smirking when they made us girls sit in the front row; they said that the Senator liked to look at pretty girls. When he arrived, I saw a slender, middle-sized, young man in a light blue suit and a handsome face. He was practically pushed into the room by two aides on either side. I had the feeling that he did not really want to be there, or, as I later learned, that he suffered of permanent pain and often needed some help with walking. He then sat down in front of us and encouraged us to ask him questions, which he all answered politely in his elegant Boston accent which reminded me a bit of the English that we had learned back in Vienna. He was friendly, but otherwise I was not deeply impressed by him.

In New York City we were taken to Harlem for a friendly chat with some Church and Community leaders. This was the first time that I actually saw and spoke with Afro-Americans, and must say from what I remember, I was very impressed by what they said.

One wonderfully warm night we were invited to a party on the beach in Long Island. We all fell asleep in the warm sand because we had been invited every night to some party, picnic, dance, or Hawaiian Luau and were exhausted. In our group of exchange students there were mostly Germans, one of them was Hilde Speer, the daughter of Hitler's famous architect, some pretty French girls, some crazy Italian boys, an elegant nobleman from Spain, a blond Frenchman from Morocco, when Morocco was still a colony of France. At the end of this month, in July 1953, we left New York Harbor on the "Independence," an Italian ship, which many years later burned down during a sea voyage. This time, I did not get seasick because the sea was quiet, and we took the southern route toward Gibraltar. As a group of 17-year-old youngsters we spent most of the time on deck and celebrated a permanent party with games, dances, making friends, and little sleep. Hilde Speer, by the way, turned out to be very nice and helpful to everybody—the thought often came to my me, that her father too may have been a gentle, good person, if he had not been fanaticized by Adolf Hitler, like so many other Germans. Another interesting person was Marianne von Reuss, the daughter from the Royal house of Reuss, a Prussian family, we called her "the Princess" which she really was. Her family lived in Garmisch-Partenkirchen, the famous Bavarian ski resort, and much later, when she was about thirty, she married the director of the Olympic Games who was at that time 90 years old. All the newspapers reported this, also that her family had become impoverished and that she needed to marry a rich guy. This is what the magazines said. I knew that she was not impoverished, but that she had become a playgirl among the international jetsetters. She was very pretty, funny, witty, and fun to be around with.

We sailed through Gibraltar into a sunny Mediterranean. By the time we arrived in Genoa, our group separated into the different nationalities and went into different directions. When we took the train from Genoa to Vienna, I was sick most of the time, probably from not having eaten properly for weeks and from lack of sleep. There was a group of Italian soldiers in our train compartment who tried to help me feel better and were generally sweet, not what one would expect from soldiers.

When we arrived in Vienna, my Oma picked me up from the train station—I must have sent her a telegram, because she did not have a telephone. Because of this lack of communication, my parents had gone on vacation to Salzburg. I was a little disappointed because by that time, I was really missing them. The next day I continued on to Salzburg, to my aunt's house at the shore of Lake Wallersee, near Salzburg, where we had already spent some wonderful vacations before. I remember that on the train ride, I got into conversations with some young people and told them about my magic year in the USA. One young man suddenly got up shouting that his heroes have always been the guys in the black suits and black boots with the swastika and skull on their shoulders. That was my first post-America experience with Nazis—many more were to come!

Even my family could not believe my wonderful experiences in America and thought that I must have been utterly brainwashed. I was! Having seen mostly the sunny sides of the USA society, I believed that indeed most people in America were middle class, most finished high school, most got good jobs right after graduation, most girls married between 19 and 22 years, that all Americans owned cars, a TV set, washing machines with dryers, a home with a garden, dishwashers, telephones, central heating, that all the schools were clean and well equipped, that many American children needed allergy shots, got the best medical care, good food and nobody in the USA was ever hungry. I had written letters to my parents every week and my mother had kept them in a bundle which I discovered after her death in one of her closets. So they were informed about my life in the USA. I was able to persuade my parents to accept an American AFS student for the rest of the summer, a girl from Topeka, Kansas, but this was not a necessary expectation by the American Field Service.

Grace was the daughter of a doctor from the University of Kansas, the very same place where I, much later, in 1969, spent time on a fellowship in the History of Medicine and wrote a paper on the Evolution of Syphilis, but more about that later.

She helped me in a way to get readjusted to Vienna by being able to speak English with her and show her around Vienna. She fitted easily into our family, although our standard of living must have been a shock to her, but she never showed it. After her departure, I had to become a real Austrian again. What I struggled with mostly, was the narrowmindedness of most people whom I tried to tell about America. They either pretended to know everything much better or confronted me with the "war crimes" that America had committed on innocent

Germans during the war. I met few people who were Pro-America, many even said that America was totally under Jewish influence, and what a pity it was that Hitler had not won the war and extinguished international "Jewery."

It was in that autumn, when my family moved into a spacious apartment within the hospital of Lainz where my father was the director of the hospital pharmacy which had to supply 4000 beds, the largest hospital in Europe. At the same time, he began to earn more money and we graduated into the upper-middle class. Lainz was a suburb of Vienna and little did I realize that it would take me more than one hour to get from Lainz to my old school and later to the University. First I had to walk to the electric train which took me to another suburb, Hietzing, from where I could take the underground or rather the overground train into the 18th district. Then I still had to take another electric train to get close to my school and then walk another ten minutes. This meant spending almost three hours on transportation and if I wanted to go to a theater in the evenings, another three hours on trains. My school expected me to graduate in 1954, so I had to make up academically for the year during which I had been in America. This meant making up all the subjects from the seventh grade in addition to keeping up with the material of the eight grade which led to graduation. It turned out that most of the material from the seventh grade was not too difficult except for Math. For that I needed a private tutor whom my parents paid for. He was a retired Math teacher, very kind, and with his help I got into advance calculus. I would be lying if I said that it was easy, but in the end, when I had to take exams for the material of the seventh grade, I got mostly "A's." I don't know how I did it, but I think that my brain had matured and it was easier for me to understand the associations. Also, my teachers had known me for so long and were a bit lenient. My classmates and all the teachers were eager to hear my reports about America. Since I had seen the USA through rose-colored lenses, few believed me and commented that I must have misunderstood what I had seen there. After all, America was the garbage pail of Europe! For the last four centuries, Europeans who were either too stupid or too lazy or too criminal would emigrate to America, kill the Natives there, grab land which belonged to the original inhabitants, and then buy themselves some slaves who would do all the heavy labor for them. These slaves built up, according to my schoolmates (remember most of them came from Nazi families!), all the industry to build railways and trains and tanks and weapons with which they eventually defeated Germany twice, in the First and in the Second World War. Now they were trying to "Americanize" Europe with their indecent films, negro music, sexual liberties, impossible political philosophies about democracy, stealing Europe's intellectuals in order to build up their nuclear arsenal and invent new technology and so on. They also made nasty comments about my clothes from America. They were all I had, such as red sweaters, long plaid skirts, one pink sweater with a pink skirt, whereas most Europeans still wore drab grey and brown nondescript clothes. Jeans and pants were not allowed in school. I did indeed look different, but my former Austrian homemade clothes I had outgrown, so I would have had to ask my parents for money to buy Austrian clothes. I had never done that before, so I continued to wear my white bobbysocks and penny loafers during the cold Viennese winter which resembles winters in Moscow. My English teacher was aghast at my American accent and when I used typical Americanisms like "you did good," she gave me a "B" in English. All in all, whereas all my teachers had liked me before America, now some of them could not deal with my new appearance and behavior.

Graduation from high school was in the summer of 1954 when I was going on 18 years. It consisted of both written and oral examinations with members of the Board of Education present. We could select the oral examinations. I selected English (needless to say), History and Geography. Because of my permanent sleep deprivation and some rather superficial understanding of things that I had missed during my year in America, I did not exactly shine at the oral exams, except for English. But in the end, my teachers were benign, understanding of my difficult circumstances, and my honest attempts to catch up by working extremely hard, and gave me mostly "A's" in the final report card.

In the weeks after this exam the entire class undertook a trip to Germany in a rented bus, the so-called "Maturareise." Everything had been meticulously arranged beforehand by all of us. We stayed in youth hostels and did all the sightseeing one can do in Germany. My AFS connections served me well now and in the near future. Almost in every German town I met with AFS students whom I had met either on the boat or the trip at the end of the year or in between at visits to New York. In the following years I did a lot of hitchhiking through Europe which was quite common and safe in those years, and again with the help of my AFS connections I was able to be invited by AFS families and saw most of western Europe, even Berlin, with almost no money in my pocket.

Soon I had to decide in which direction I wanted to go in life. I had always been pretty good in everything, but not outstanding in anything. I could have gone to the University studying anything except for Math or Engineering; I even considered the Academy of Art, but who knows at the age of 17 whether one is really talented enough in Art. So, in order to postpone this decision, I first went to the American Embassy and applied for a job there. After all, I knew how to type and speak English fluently! When I filled out my application forms, the staff suddenly started laughing, because I was not yet 18 years old and they can employ people only after their 18th birthday. On August 31, my birthday, I began the first real job in my life.

I was assigned to an American general whose office was in the former Franz Josef Train Station which had been bombed out and not yet rebuilt except for some office rooms. I was of course as beginner the lowest on the pecking order. I worked in an office together with two Viennese women who were both engaged to be married to American GIs. I learned soon that clerical work was boring and not at all challenging. After all, I had just passed exams in college level calculus and philosophy. My typing was not that great, but that can be learned, but the content of the letters was boring, the conversations in the office were of such low class that I could not even participate. When word spread that a young woman like me had just joined the General's office, the U.S. soldiers constantly hung around our windows to take a look at me, something that the other women in the office disliked grimly. I soon told the General that I would leave and enroll at the university. He was a small, thin man, supposedly without humor and a chain-smoker. He had been in the Second World War and in Korea, probably was a war hero—I liked him and regret to this day that I have forgotten his name.

He was the only person who showed genuine regret for losing me, but also said that he understood completely why I needed to go on to the University and hope that I would become a great scientist or philosopher or doctor.

At that time, I lived in my grandparents' apartment in the 9th district, within walking distance to my job and to the University. Their apartment was tiny, consisting only of a kitchen without a window, no bathroom, one living/bedroom, one extra room where my mother had slept, and my Opa's studio where he repaired shoes together with one or two helpers. When my mother's brother, Uncle Hans, lived at home, he had to sleep in the shoe studio and do his homework at school. This apartment was so dark that one could not see the sky and therefore not know about the weather. The extra room could not be heated, it was only meant for sleeping. My studying I was supposed to do at the University library which would have been possible.

I still did not know in which Faculty to enroll and tried out lectures in economics, law, languages, all of which I enjoyed. I wasted almost one semester in this way, when suddenly I ran into my old friend Guenther Pernhaupt from the AFS in the street near the Anatomic Institute. He was happy to see me and so was I. He immediately invited me to go with him to see the Medical School where he was enrolled. He wanted to show me the autopsy room where he was working at that time. I think he also wanted to show me off to his friends as "his girlfriend." It boosted his self-esteem enormously when he suddenly showed up with a girl in a tight red sweater and lipstick. There was no end to the astonishment harvested by Guenther, particularly when he told his friends that I had been an AFS student together with him, and therefore smart too. I felt very welcome at Medical School and—thank God—decided quickly that without enrolling immediately in medicine, I was just wasting my time and that I had found a home. It was easy to do that, all I had to do was go to the Dean's office and fill out papers and show my graduation certificate which was so good that no questions were asked. I had, of course, previously considered medicine, but was a little afraid of the responsibilities and decisions a doctor had to make about people's lives or death. I had to quickly make up for the time I had lost by just loitering around and quickly began studying as hard as I could.

There was a study room at the Institute of Anatomy, which we called the "Bone Chamber." There one could sit all day and study anatomical preparations, the bones with joints and look at the mechanics of the ligaments and tendons. And this room was even heated! I had truly found my real home! In order to begin the Dissecting Exercises, one had to pass the so-called "Bone Colloquium" first. This was at the same time the first major filtering process for the students. In Vienna, it is not hard to enroll in Medicine, no entrance exams, nothing, just having graduated from a high school. So it can happen that too many students enroll in Medicine, students who may not necessarily make good doctors in the end, or take up the places of more appropriate candidates. In addition to Austrian high school graduates, there were many foreign students from third-world countries who enrolled at the University of Vienna, and clearly there is not room for everybody. Tuition is completely free for Austrian students except for a minor enrollment fee. Foreign students have to pay a minor tuition, but no comparison to a U.S. Medical School! So we ended up even with a number of U.S. students who could not afford the tuition fees in the USA. But we also had many students from Iran, the Arabic and African countries, from India and Israel. Austria considered giving a good education to third-world students as its way of giving foreign aid to these countries. I ended up spending much time in the "Bone Chamber" because I had already lost almost one semester and had to catch up with my colleagues such as Guenther. Other students were very helpful, one could ask anybody for help. These bone mechanics are not easy to understand! I literally threw myself into studying hard again and soon passed this colloquium (an oral examination) with an "A." I had noticed some extremely pretty girls enrolling in Medical School and the male students just waiting for them to fail the bone colloquium, because we all thought that some of these girls had enrolled in Medicine only in order to catch a young doctor for marriage. This became a big joke among us, but sometimes the male students were wrong. Now the more enjoyable part began by attending classes in physics, chemistry, anatomy, physiology in the mornings and in the afternoons until late night dissecting body parts in the dissecting room. There was a large group of students from all over the world tutored by older students. Initially we studied mostly the muscles, ligaments, nerves, arteries and veins. Sometimes one of the assistant professors came in and questioned us about the names of the different parts that we were dissecting. There is so much to remember in Anatomy, and rote learning had never been my forte, but I tried to pursue my original goal which was to graduate from Medical School "sus auspicis Presidentis," which means that the president of the Republic would be present at my graduation because I had passed every examination with an "A" which was very rare. Within a few months I had caught up with everybody else in this class, passed all my exams with an "A" and at the same time enjoyed myself immensely.

One problem remained. I still lived with my grandparents and only went home on weekends for a bath and a hot meal. Since my Oma did not have a bathroom, I could not wash up well after the dissecting exercises. I guess that soon all my clothes smelled of dead corpses, but so did everybody else's. We were given small lockers where we could have exchanged our clothes, but it was difficult for girls to undress in front of the boys, and even these lockers smelled bad. So I went to classical concerts, stage theaters, and to the opera quite frequently in innocent unawareness. On the other hand, so many people smoked in Europe, particularly all the medical students, that I probably still smelled better than the rest of them because I never got into the habit of smoking. The dissecting rooms were large classrooms fitted with some forty tables and four students to each table. We helped each other as much as possible. During these exercises I got to know many students from interesting countries, and some had a hard time with the German language. When they found out that I spoke English fluently, the students from the Arabic countries soon came to me for help. They came mostly from Egypt, but also some from Pakistan and Iraq. Practically all of them came from medical families, were well educated, and very friendly, social, intelligent, and eager to learn more about Vienna. At that time, after my year in America, I was also interested in getting to know people from all other countries and soon I was invited by the Egyptians to come to their Ramadan dinners late at night when they were allowed to eat for the first time in the day during the Ramadan month of fasting. My best friends among the Egyptians were Anwar el Hagin from Alexandria, Ezra and Mahfous from Cairo. Anwar's mother was from Vienna and so he could live with his grandparents, not too far away from the University. He was a real sweetheart and much later he often came to my house in order for me to tutor him. Ezra had difficulties with physics, so he asked me to give him private lessons which I did, but I was only one chapter ahead of him each time. Finally after passing his exam successfully he wanted to pay me, but I refused to accept money from a colleague. So he brought me after the summer a beautiful necklace from Egypt, an antique as seen on the Egyptian grave inscriptions. Mahfous eventually graduated "sub Auspicis Presidentis" in Vienna and was given a red carpet welcome by President Nasser when he arrived back in Egypt and probably a great job right from the beginning. He deserved it! The Indians and Pakistanis rarely approached me, they stayed in their own groups. Also I think that they were all married by the time they arrived in Vienna according to their traditions. I remember one Egyptian who was darker than the Arabic Egyptians, he was a Coptic, a descendant of the ancient Pharaohs. He was very elegant and smart. Some of the African students were also very likeable, friendly, and very good students. I remember once after an examination, the Professor stood up and bowed to this little African student saying: "Please promise me to go back to your own country when you are done here, because there they need people like you very badly!" We also had some Kurdish, many Greek, and Filipino students and many from Iran, even some girls from Iran. The Iranian students were a mixed lot. One could tell by the way they dressed in expensive fur coats in the winters that they had received scholarships from the Shah of Persia. We were even warned to be careful with them, because some were probably members of the Shah's feared secret police force, sent to Vienna in order to spy upon their fellow countrymen.

It was here at the Medical School where I met Katja. She was enrolled for a while, but never passed any exams, and soon dropped out. Still we became good friends—her talents were in more linguistic directions. She was from the borderland between Austria and Slowenia, spoke Slowenic at home which was a large farm, spoke German in school, but also spoke Russian, French, Italian, some Spanish, in addition to having learned ancient Greek in high school. She was very pretty, charming, and well liked. In the summer of 1955, she invited me and another girl from my school in Vienna, Erika Molisch, to spend the summer vacation at her farm in a little village where everybody spoke Slowenic. She had spent her childhood in a concentration camp, simply for one reason, for being Slawic, and it was there where her older sister was euthanized with an injection by an SS doctor, because she had developed a little fever. Erika Molisch was the daughter of a famous university professor in biology, but he had become a Nazi, in order to stay at the university, and so after the war, the family became very poor. Erika was in my class in high school and in the summer camps, where she would always sit next to me, because she was always hungry, and I could easily and happily share my meals with her. Her family was actually one of the few who was punished after the war for being Nazi. I am reporting these things only to show how little prejudiced Katja was. Her parents were rich farmers with horses and even a diesel engine for threshing and other agricultural work. Next to their huge farm there was a fishpond, which to me looked like the most beautiful swimming pool surrounded by flowers and with clear, clean water. We actually ended up spending a lot of time in that swimming pool. She also invited my latest "conquest," an Israeli medical student, Paul Rudich and his friend Gad Gutman. Israeli students were older than we were and much more mature, because they had to train in the Israeli Military, before they were allowed to go abroad to study. His father had been a popular doctor in Vienna. He himself was born in Vienna and one could hear from his German that he had been born in Vienna! After Hitler had arrived in Vienna with his Army, a patient of Dr. Rudich, an SS man at that time, ran over to Dr. Rudich's home and told him to immediately pack up and leave Vienna with the last train to Italy, lest the Gestapo was going to pick up the entire family within a few hours. It seems that there is such a thing as a patient's gratefulness to his doctor! The Rudich family finally arrived in Tell Aviv where they settled down and Dr. Rudich continued a thriving medical practice. Pauli was not only very good looking, very athletic, but also completely decent, honest, and reliable. He had been an officer in the Israeli Airforce before he came to Vienna and had begun research with some fish and could be found in the Biology Lab most of the time. He was about 23 years old, whereas I was barely 19, so I looked up to him as a mature man. As a boy already he had been helping out in the Israeli Army in their first war against the surrounding Arabic countries, by carrying ammunition and guns into the frontlines. Gad, on the other hand, was interested in Katja. He was so smart that I was in awe of him. Some other friends of Katja soon joined us at the fishpond and it turned out that this summer became probably the best summer of my life. Pauli introduced me to hitchhiking, which was done by most students with little money and it was much safer then. Fewer people owned cars then and so people without cars in the rural areas were given rides by people with cars. Even Katja's family did not own a car. When we arrived by train in the town with the nearest train station, Katja picked us up with a horse wagon and sometimes, when we went into the city to go dancing we took the horse wagon there. We still giggle thinking how we went dancing in a wagon, not even in an elegant horse carriage! Katja told me another story from the war, which sounds almost like a fable from the Old Testament: One of her relatives, a young woman, was assigned to a high Nazi officer/politician as a housemaid, as many Slowenic women were. This Nazi family, however, began to like the charming, pretty, and intelligent girl so much that they became friends. The officer/politician warned her that Hitler's ultimate plan was to destroy all the Slawic peoples, except for those who were to become slaves on the estates of Germany, which were to be established after the "final victory" in Russia. It seems that this family finally decided that Slowenic people are "better" Slawic people, and that they should not be destroyed like the Jews and the Gypsies.

1955-1956

During the next semester, a solution was found concerning my living situation. At my grandparents' apartment I could really not study because my room was very cold most of the time. On Sundays the medical study room and libraries were closed. It was like a little miracle when my mother told me that she had found a room for me near the Medical School which would also be inexpensive, particularly if I would be willing to share it with a roommate. This room was in a two-bedroom apartment within easy walking distance of the Medical School. It belonged to an elderly lady who needed the second bedroom only sometimes when she visited her apartment from the small town where she had moved to. I happily jumped at this opportunity. There were even two beds in that room and a large desk in front of a window with a nice view of a baroque church and trees. The rent for this room was 300 shillings, the equivalent of perhaps 300 Euros today. If I shared it with a roommate, I could easily pay 150 shillings rent and use the remaining 150 shillings from my parents for food and other expenses. It was easy to find a roommate for such a low-priced room. Edda turned out to be an ideal roommate. She was never there. She had found a boyfriend with whom she moved in, but wanted to keep our place just in case. So I ended up living almost alone, the first time in my life, and I could go out in the evenings without fear of missing the last train at night. Also I could use the desk next to the window for studying. There was no stove or any heating system in that room, like in most rented rooms in Vienna, but my mother gave me a small electric heater which kept my legs warm when sitting at the desk and wearing my warmest clothes, I could manage and study late at night when even the university library was closed. And on Sundays I could study all day long without interruption and soon passed some other examinations with "A's." The most difficult exam at that time was considered to be chemistry, which included biochemistry. It was so much feared that it was considered to be the next filtering system and many students who could not pass it for the second time, had to drop out of Medical School. I passed that too with a straight "A." After this, my colleagues became more respectful of me and even started inviting me to their socials and I gave parties at my parents large apartment. Before that, the typical Xenophobic attitude of many Austrians, particularly that of the Neo-Nazis, prevented them from socializing with me because I had been seen socializing with so many foreigners. I had never imagined that there were some who could and would never forgive me for having a Jewish boyfriend. Unfortunately, this relationship broke up sadly, partially because my family would never have accepted a Jewish man into our family and his family in Tell Aviv likewise would not have accepted me with their own terrible experience in Vienna after Hitler's marching into Austria.

The Neo-Nazis at Medical School planned a dirty revenge for me, also perhaps because I was seen as too ambitious for a girl. How could they really hurt me and possibly remove me as a competitor? Much later I heard rumors that they plotted the following: One of the best-looking, blond, young gods, a fanatical Nazi and great athlete, offered to become my next "boyfriend." We had often seen each other in classes and I had no idea that he belonged to those fanatics. He began sitting next to me and later we happened to be in a dissecting class together which dealt exclusively with the brain. Very interesting! But at that time, in 1956, only the names of the various brain structures were known, hardly anything about their function. I wanted very much to know if the brain of Schizophrenics was in any way different anatomically or histologically from that of normal people. A good colleague of ours, a real sweetheart, had suddenly become schizophrenic, after failing some examinations. Later he became a patient of Guenther Pernhaupt, my friend from the Queen Mary on the way to the USA in 1952, and who had convinced me that I should go into Medicine for which I had not needed much persuasion. At that time I knew already that I should become a psychiatrist. Siegfried, who was to become my new boyfriend, started inviting me to dinners—apparently he had much more money than I. We also went together to watch some interesting political films and to poetry readings. Siegfried turned out to be a great admirer of one contemporary poet in Vienna who also happened to have been a great Nazi, but I did not know that. He made me read the book about the "Elders of Zion," a famous Russian fantasy about the International Jewry planning and conspiring to conquer the entire western world not only economically, but also politically. I was warned by Katja that this book is well known and was one of the favorite pieces of literature in the Nazi world to warn the Germans of the real and immense danger that International Jewry was capable of. I began to suspect that this young man was trying to persuade me that Hitler had not been all that bad. At the age of less than twenty years and mostly preoccupied with my next medical examinations, I did not understand enough history or politics or human relationships to recognize that this handsome young man was a dangerous Nazi and was, as I later understood, to become one member of the future German Fascist leadership. I had never in my life before met a person without any conscience and he was truly evil. I had only read stories about evil people or had seen films about the evil that had been committed during the war on all sides. It was a beautiful May with prematurely warm evenings when we could go for long walks and I fell in love magically. I experienced a feeling that I had never known before, I longed to be in his presence and to be with him. Then he raped me. And it was the first time in my life! After that night I did not see him for a long time because he travelled back home to Salzburg the next day and I soon went to a summer camp with the America Field Service in Belgium and did some hitchhiking all the way into Berlin, which was at that time seriously divided into a grey, colorless east and a blossoming west with Russian soldiers watching the border between east and west Berlin. At that time there was no Berlin Wall yet, but the famous "checkpoint Charlie."

Back in Austria, near Salzburg, I contacted Siegfried and we planned on meeting in the city. I had assumed that he would introduce me to his family or some friends, as many of my colleagues had introduced me to their Arabic or Iranian families because they were proud of knowing me. Siegfried instead took me on his motorcycle and roamed with me through the countryside where nobody could see us. I instinctively felt that he did not want to be seen with me, he was ashamed of me. He had done his job of raping me, for which he was certainly congratulated by his buddies. I never saw him again. I am sure that he finished Medical School, but Fate had a different plan for my life. As much as Adolf Hitler had believed in his Destiny, the goddesses of Fate may have been persuaded by His Muse of Fate to send me off into a different direction.

www.ingramcontent.com/pod-product-compliance
Lightning Source LLC
Chambersburg PA
CBHW061705120626
46550CB00003B/1102